OPRAH
WINFREY

WOMEN of ACHIEVEMENT

OPRAH WINFREY

Belinda Friedrich

CHELSEA HOUSE PUBLISHERS
PHILADELPHIA

Frontispiece: Popular talk-show host Oprah Winfrey overcame poverty and abuse to become one of the most influential and admired people in America.

PRODUCED BY 21st Century Publishing and Communications, Inc., New York, N.Y.

Chelsea House Publishers
EDITOR IN CHIEF Sally Cheney
ASSOCIATE EDITOR IN CHIEF Kim Shinners
PRODUCTION MANAGER Pamela Loos
ART DIRECTOR Sara Davis
DIRECTOR OF PHOTOGRAPHY Judy L. Hasday
Cover Designer Terry Mallon

The Chelsea House World Wide Web address is
http://www.chelseahouse.com

3 5 7 9 8 6 4 2

Library of Congress Cataloging-in-Publication Data

Friedrich, Belinda.
Oprah Winfrey / Belinda Friedrich.
  p. cm. — (Women of achievement)
Includes bibliographical references and index.
Summary: A biography of the popular talk show host who rose from a childhood of poverty to become one of the most visible women in the nation.
ISBN 0-7910-5891-3 — ISBN 0-7910-5892-1 (pbk.)
1. Winfrey, Oprah—Juvenile literature. 2. Television personalities—United States—Biography—Juvenile literature. 3. Women television personalities—United States—Biography—Juvenile literature. 4. Motion picture actors and actresses—United States—Biography—Juvenile literature. 5. Actresses—United States—Biography—Juvenile literature. [1. Winfrey, Oprah. 2. Television personalities. 3. Actors and actresses. 4. Women—Biography. 5. Afro-Americans—Biography.] I. Title. II. Series.

PN1992.4.W56 F75 2000
791.45′028′092—dc21
[B]   00-021511

CONTENTS

"Remember the Ladies"—Matina S. Horner   7

1. *The Color Purple*   13

2. The "Talkingest" Child   17

3. Getting It Together   27

4. The Talk of the Town   39

5. *The Oprah Winfrey Show*   53

6. Confronting Tough Issues   71

7. At the Top of Her Game   87

8. New Worlds to Conquer   97

Chronology   102

Awards   104

Bibliography   105

Index   108

WOMEN of ACHIEVEMENT

Jane Addams
SOCIAL WORKER

Madeleine Albright
STATESWOMAN

Marian Anderson
SINGER

Susan B. Anthony
WOMAN SUFFRAGIST

Clara Barton
AMERICAN RED CROSS FOUNDER

Margaret Bourke-White
PHOTOGRAPHER

Rachel Carson
BIOLOGIST AND AUTHOR

Cher
SINGER AND ACTRESS

Hillary Rodham Clinton
FIRST LADY AND ATTORNEY

Katie Couric
JOURNALIST

Diana, Princess of Wales
HUMANITARIAN

Emily Dickinson
POET

Elizabeth Dole
POLITICIAN

Amelia Earhart
AVIATOR

Gloria Estefan
SINGER

Jodie Foster
ACTRESS AND DIRECTOR

Betty Friedan
FEMINIST

Althea Gibson
TENNIS CHAMPION

Ruth Bader Ginsburg
SUPREME COURT JUSTICE

Helen Hayes
ACTRESS

Katharine Hepburn
ACTRESS

Mahalia Jackson
GOSPEL SINGER

Helen Keller
HUMANITARIAN

**Ann Landers/
Abigail Van Buren**
COLUMNISTS

Barbara McClintock
BIOLOGIST

Margaret Mead
ANTHROPOLOGIST

Edna St. Vincent Millay
POET

Julia Morgan
ARCHITECT

Toni Morrison
AUTHOR

Grandma Moses
PAINTER

Lucretia Mott
WOMAN SUFFRAGIST

Sandra Day O'Connor
SUPREME COURT JUSTICE

Rosie O'Donnell
ENTERTAINER AND COMEDIAN

Georgia O'Keeffe
PAINTER

Eleanor Roosevelt
DIPLOMAT AND HUMANITARIAN

Wilma Rudolph
CHAMPION ATHLETE

Elizabeth Cady Stanton
WOMAN SUFFRAGIST

Harriet Beecher Stowe
AUTHOR AND ABOLITIONIST

Barbra Streisand
ENTERTAINER

Elizabeth Taylor
ACTRESS AND ACTIVIST

Mother Teresa
HUMANITARIAN AND
RELIGIOUS LEADER

Barbara Walters
JOURNALIST

Edith Wharton
AUTHOR

Phillis Wheatley
POET

Oprah Winfrey
ENTERTAINER

Babe Didrikson Zaharias
CHAMPION ATHLETE

"REMEMBER THE LADIES"

MATINA S. HORNER

"Remember the Ladies." That is what Abigail Adams wrote to her husband John, then a delegate to the Continental Congress, as the Founding Fathers met in Philadelphia to form a new nation in March of 1776. "Be more generous and favorable to them than your ancestors. Do not put such unlimited power in the hands of the Husbands. If particular care and attention is not paid to the Ladies," Abigail Adams warned, "we are determined to foment a Rebellion, and will not hold ourselves bound by any Laws in which we have no voice, or Representation."

The words of Abigail Adams, one of the earliest American advocates of women's rights, were prophetic. Because when we have not "remembered the ladies," they have, by their words and deeds, reminded us so forcefully of the omission that we cannot fail to remember them. For the history of American women is as interesting and varied as the history of our nation as a whole. American women have played an integral part in founding, settling, and building our country. Some we remember as remarkable women who—against great odds—achieved distinction in the public arena: Anne Hutchinson, who in the 17th century became a charismatic religious leader; Phillis Wheatley, an 18th-century black slave who became a poet; Susan B. Anthony, whose name is synonymous with the 19th-century women's rights movement, and who led the struggle to enfranchise women; and in the 20th century, Amelia Earhart, the first woman to cross the Atlantic Ocean by air.

These extraordinary women certainly merit our admiration, but other women, "common women," many of them all but forgotten, should also be recognized for their contributions to American thought and culture. Women have been community builders; they have founded schools and formed voluntary associations to help those in need; they have assumed the major responsibility for rearing children, passing on from one generation to the next the values that keep a culture alive. These and innumerable other contributions, once ignored, are now being recognized by scholars, students, and the public. It is exciting and gratifying that a part of our history that was hardly acknowledged a few generations ago is now being studied and brought to light.

In recent decades, the field of women's history has grown from obscurity to a politically controversial splinter movement to academic respectability, in many cases mainstreamed into such traditional disciplines as history, economics, and psychology. Scholars of women, both female and male, have organized research centers at such prestigious institutions as Wellesley College, Stanford University, and the University of California. Other notable centers for women's studies are the Center for the American Woman and Politics at the Eagleton Institute of Politics at Rutgers University; the Henry A. Murray Research Center for the Study of Lives, at Radcliffe College; and the Women's Research and Education Institute, the research arm of the Congressional Caucus on Women's Issues. Other scholars and public figures have established archives and libraries, such as the Schlesinger Library on the History of Women in America, at Radcliffe College, and the Sophia Smith Collection, at Smith College, to collect and preserve the written and tangible legacies of women.

From the initial donation of the Women's Rights Collection in 1943, the Schlesinger Library grew to encompass vast collections documenting the manifold accomplishments of American women. Simultaneously, the women's movement in general and the academic discipline of women's studies in particular also began with a narrow definition and gradually expanded their mandate. Early causes, such as woman suffrage and social reform, abolition, and organized labor were joined by newer concerns, such as the history of women in business and the professions and in politics and government; the study of the family; and social issues such as health policy and education.

Women, as historian Arthur M. Schlesinger, jr., once pointed out, "have constituted the most spectacular casualty of traditional history. They have made up at least half the human race, but you could never tell that by looking at the books historians write." The new breed of historians is remedying that omission. They have written books about immigrant women and about working-class women who struggled for survival in cities and about black women who met the challenges of life in rural areas. They are telling the stories of women who, despite the barriers of tradition and economics, became lawyers and doctors and public figures.

The women's studies movement has also led scholars to question traditional interpretations of their respective disciplines. For example, the study of war has traditionally been an exercise in military and political analysis, an examination of strategies planned and executed by men. But scholars of women's history have pointed out that wars have also been periods of tremendous change and even opportunity for women, because the very absence of men on the home front enabled them to expand their educational, economic, and professional activities and to assume leadership in their homes.

The early scholars of women's history showed a unique brand of courage in choosing to investigate new subjects and take new approaches to old ones. Often, like their subjects, they endured criticism and even ostracism by their academic colleagues. But their efforts have unquestionably been worthwhile, because with the publication of each new study and book another piece of the historical patchwork is sewn into place, revealing an increasingly comprehensive picture of the role of women in our rich and varied history.

Such books on groups of women are essential, but books that focus on the lives of individuals are equally indispensable. Biographies can be inspirational, offering their readers the example of people with vision who have looked outside themselves for their goals and have often struggled against great obstacles to achieve them. Marian Anderson, for instance, had to overcome racial bigotry in order to perfect her art and perform as a concert singer. Isadora Duncan defied the rules of classical dance to find true artistic freedom. Jane Addams had to break down society's notions of the proper role for women in order to create new social situations, notably the settlement house. All of these women had to come to terms both with themselves and with the world in which they lived. Only then could they move ahead as pioneers in their chosen callings.

Biography can inspire not only by adulation but also by realism. It helps us to see not only the qualities in others that we hope to emulate, but also, perhaps, the weaknesses that made them "human." By helping us identify with the subject on a more personal level they help us feel that we, too, can achieve such goals. We read about Eleanor Roosevelt, for instance, who occupied a unique and seemingly enviable position as the wife of the president. Yet we can sympathize with her inner dilemma; an inherently shy woman, she had to force herself to live a most public life in order to use her position to benefit others. We may not be able to imagine ourselves having the immense poetic talent of Emily Dickinson, but from her story we can understand the challenges faced by a creative woman who was expected to fulfill many family responsibilities. And though few of us will ever reach the level of athletic accomplishment displayed by Wilma Rudolph or Babe Zaharias, we can still appreciate their spirit, their overwhelming will to excel.

A biography is a multifaceted lens. It is first of all a magnification, the intimate examination of one particular life. But at the same time, it is a wide-angle lens, informing us about the world in which the subject lived. We come away from reading about one life knowing more about the social, political, and economic fabric of the time. It is for this reason, perhaps, that the great New England essayist Ralph Waldo Emerson wrote in 1841, "There is properly no history: only biography." And it is also why biography, and particularly women's biography, will continue to fascinate writers and readers alike.

Oprah earned an Oscar nomination as Best Supporting Actress for her first film role as Sofia in The Color Purple. *In this scene from the film she appears with costar Willard Pugh, who played her husband, Harpo.*

1

THE COLOR PURPLE

arly in 1985, in Chicago, Illinois, millions of viewers were watching their favorite local morning television talk show, *A.M. Chicago.* They followed closely as the show's popular host, 31-year-old Oprah Winfrey, interviewed a guest. Among the Chicago television viewers that day was a stranger in town, a man sitting in a hotel room. The man was Quincy Jones, the famous musical producer, traveling on business. Although Jones was not aware of the host's name, he was very impressed by her warmth and charm. In this young African-American woman he immediately saw the image of Sofia, a supporting character in Alice Walker's novel *The Color Purple.* Jones was coproducer of an upcoming major motion picture based on Walker's Pulitzer Prize–winning book, and he was convinced he had just found the perfect candidate for the role of Sofia.

Jones quickly found out the woman's name and personal details and passed the information on to Reuben Cannon, the movie's casting director. That was all it took for the local talk-show host to be asked to audition for a role in one of 1985's most anticipated movies.

Oprah had never appeared in anything other than college stage productions, but by all accounts her audition was a huge success. Director Steven Spielberg reportedly told the hopeful actress that she was ideal for the role, but he would have to audition other people before he would make his final decision.

Oprah returned to Chicago and tried to focus instead on a bet to lose weight that she had recently made with comedian Joan Rivers. The talk-show host was so serious about winning the bet that she visited a health farm in Gilman, Illinois. While at the farm, Oprah received a call from Reuben Cannon, informing her that she had won the role of Sofia. The young woman was ecstatic.

Then Cannon asked Oprah what she was doing at the farm. "Losing weight! I'm on a diet! Congratulate me," said a giddy Oprah.

"You're playing Sofia!" he responded. "You can't lose weight! Whatever you've lost, you'd better go out and find it again." Not only did Oprah have to gain back what she'd lost, but she also had to put on enough additional weight to wear a size 18 dress for the role.

Before she could officially accept the part, Oprah had to negotiate with her employer so that she could take six weeks off that summer for filming *The Color Purple*. The actual shooting ended up taking twice that long.

Making the movie was a tremendous opportunity for the inexperienced actress. She worked with a stellar cast, including Laurence Fishburne, Danny Glover, and Whoopie Goldberg. Alice Walker herself attended many days of the filming. When the last scene was shot, Oprah returned to life in Chicago, but she could hardly wait for the film's release later that year.

The Color Purple opened on December 18, 1985, to mixed reviews from critics. Most reviewers praised the acting, especially that of Oprah, but felt that the story was unfair to black men in its portrayal of their abusive behavior toward women.

In spite of the lackluster reviews, when Academy Award nominations were announced later that winter, *The Color Purple* was recognized in 11 categories. Oprah was nominated for Best Supporting Actress. On Oscar night, however, the movie did not win a single award.

Oprah remained gratified to be honored with an Oscar nomination in her first film role. Her experience with *The Color Purple* showed her the power of the visual arts to highlight relevant and sometimes controversial social issues.

Oprah has used that power of the media to help others overcome problems that she has faced, and many of the projects she takes on deal with important social issues. Her daily television show, her magazine, and her movies address subjects such as broken relationships, sexual abuse, bigotry, and rejection. Oprah also focuses on personal development, using her influence to offer people ways to grow as individuals and improve their lives.

A desire to help others drives Oprah's career. She understands that she herself has a unique platform from which to make a difference in people's lives. "In a society so media controlled," she has said, "doing good film is one of the best ways to raise consciousness." As head of a multimillion-dollar media company, Oprah Winfrey is taking every opportunity to do just that.

But early achievements, like her role in *The Color Purple*, brought a more personal reward to Oprah as well: her father's praise. "Oprah has come further than I ever thought of her going," Vernon Winfrey said after viewing the movie. "She's come a long way. See, I can look back and see from where she came and I am proud that she made it."

Oprah's accomplishments are an amazing feat for a woman who was once a lonely little girl enduring incredible suffering and rejection.

As a young child, Oprah lived with her grandparents on their small farm in rural Mississippi. Like the old farmhouse shown here, Oprah's childhood home had no indoor plumbing.

2

THE "TALKINGEST" CHILD

On January 29, 1954, a tiny baby who would become famous for her gift of gab was born in the small, central Mississippi town of Kosciusko. The baby's great-aunt Ida was given the honor of naming the new family member. Ida intended to name the baby Orpah, after a woman in the Bible, but the letters were transposed on the birth certificate and "Orpah" became "Oprah."

Oprah's hometown was named in honor of Tadeusz Andrzei Bonawentura Kościuszko, a Polish general who served with George Washington in the American Revolutionary War. He was famous for his struggles to bring freedom to all people—including slaves. While the Mississippi town may have been named for the Polish reformer, its residents did not seem to share his ideals. Laws in the rural town kept African Americans from voting and maintained separate schools and other public places for blacks and whites.

When Vernita Lee, a single African-American woman, gave birth to her baby girl, few people paid much attention. The baby's father, Vernon Winfrey, didn't even know that he had a daughter. Serving in the army, he had met Vernita while on leave from Fort Rucker, Alabama, and the young couple barely knew each other. Oprah later said that her birth was the result of "a one-day fling under an oak tree." Vernita did not tell Vernon that she became pregnant, and no one else in the small Mississippi town bothered to send the news to the young man living in Alabama.

Vernon finally heard about his child shortly after her birth when Vernita wrote to him, but apparently they made no arrangements for him to provide child support. Years later, he said, "I am not proud of what happened with Oprah's mother and me." He added, "I tell people today that if something like this happens, the boy should help take care of the child."

Vernita faced many problems as an unwed mother. Not only was she young and a member of a persecuted minority but she also lived in a town facing serious economic hardship. The local cotton mill, which had employed most of the townspeople, had shut down, putting thousands of people out of work. It soon became impossible to find any employment in Kosciusko, and almost 6,000 workers left town to find jobs elsewhere. But Vernita came from a large family, whose members were willing to do what they could to help her out.

Vernita's parents, Earless (pronounced Urliss) and Hattie Mae Lee, took the new baby to live with them on their small farm. Hattie Mae worked as a cook for the sheriff and took in laundry, and Earless grew vegetables and raised animals to make a living. For young Oprah, life on a small Mississippi farm was difficult. She had no friends her own age to play with, and she had plenty of work to do. Her grandmother urged the little girl to watch her do laundry and learn how to boil clothes because she would someday have to earn a living that way. While Oprah obeyed her grandmother, she was determined to carve out a different life for herself. She later told an interviewer that when her grandmother said she would grow up to do laundry, she thought, "Oh, no I'm not."

Stories about Oprah's years growing up on her grandparents' farm differ depending upon who is recalling the events. Oprah Winfrey has said that she did chores on the farm, including tending to the animals and drawing water from a well because the house had no indoor plumbing. However, Oprah's cousin Katherine Carr Esters remembers life on the farm a bit differently. She has stated that "[Oprah] was treated like a little princess and grew up in a house with a bunch of grown folks who doted on her." Even Oprah's mother has said that her daughter "toots it up a little" when remembering her years on the farm, and probably overdramatizes many of these memories. While Oprah may exaggerate the amount of work in those early years, farm life has never been known as luxurious. Clearly, growing up in a small rural town was not easy for the little girl.

Church provided Oprah and the rest of her family with some social life. It also gave neighbors the first glimpse of the natural talent the young girl had for entertaining people. In 1957 Oprah supposedly had her first public speaking experience when she gave a recitation of the story of Jesus in her local church on Easter Sunday. The adult parishioners loved it, but other children seemed to envy the attention that the precocious three-year-old garnered from being involved in the program. Oprah recalled in an interview that other church members would tell her grandmother, "This child sure can talk. She is the talkingest child."

Oprah could not only talk well at an early age but also read and write. When the little girl entered kindergarten, she had already acquired the reading and writing skills that the other children were just beginning to learn. She soon found schoolwork boring and decided to take action. The kindergartner sat down and wrote a letter to her teacher explaining that she didn't think she belonged in the class. Once her teacher read Oprah's letter, she advanced the little girl to first grade. The young student's abilities amazed the school administrators, who later moved her into a third-grade classroom.

In 1960, when Oprah turned six, her grandparents decided that caring for the energetic little girl was more than they could cope with, so they contacted her mother. Two years earlier Vernita Lee had moved to Milwaukee, Wisconsin, where she was working as a maid in the suburbs. While life was not easy, she managed to make ends meet with some supplemental help from the state's social welfare program. Vernita had also met a man who had promised to marry her, so she agreed to take over the care of her daughter. Oprah was sent to Milwaukee. Years later Oprah commented that she didn't know why her mother ever decided to take her. "She wasn't equipped to take care of me," Oprah said. "I was just an extra burden on her."

If life on a southern farm had presented problems for Oprah, life in the urban north proved just as hard. The young child arrived in Milwaukee to discover that she had a half-sister, Patricia. Shortly after Oprah arrived, her half-brother, Jeffrey, was born. Vernita's marriage did not take place, but one of her boyfriend's relatives allowed the family to move into a single room of their house.

Oprah found refuge from the chaos of her family life by reading. She also gave recitations at church and in social clubs. Unlike Oprah's grandparents, Vernita did not praise the young girl for excelling at school and for loving books. Vernita once told her, "You think you're better than the other kids." Oprah later recalled, "I was treated as though something was wrong with me because I wanted to read all the time." Other children teased her for being "bookish."

Life in Milwaukee was not what Oprah had expected, and the reunion between mother and daughter was not turning out like either one had hoped. After two years,

Vernita called Oprah's father to see if he would be willing to care for their daughter. Vernon Winfrey had been discharged from the military in 1955 and had a stable job as a maintenance worker at Vanderbilt University in Nashville, Tennessee. He had married and settled down in a small house with his wife, Zelma. Vernon Winfrey agreed to take Oprah, and in 1962, the eight-year-old girl found herself living with her father and stepmother.

By all accounts, Vernon and Zelma Winfrey provided Oprah with a stable home life. They both valued education, and Oprah's interest in books was not discouraged the way it had been while she was living with her mother. Discipline and order were Oprah's guiding principles of life in Nashville. She has said that living with the Winfreys was like being in a military school. Once Zelma discovered that her stepdaughter did not know her multiplication tables, the woman devoted an entire summer to teaching them to the young girl. Studying multiplication tables wasn't the only thing that interrupted Oprah's free time during summer vacation; she also had to do book reports and learn new vocabulary words each week.

Oprah also benefited from the Winfreys' active involvement in a local church. Both her father and stepmother were very religious. They encouraged Oprah to memorize religious and inspirational passages, and the girl recited the writings at church and at church-related functions.

Back in Milwaukee, Vernita still clung to the hope that she was going to get married soon, and she wanted to have all her children living together with her when she did. In 1963, she asked Vernon to let Oprah come to Milwaukee for the summer. Vernon and Zelma had settled Oprah into a routine family life, but they reluctantly took the girl back to her mother, with the understanding that the visit was just for the summer. When Vernon returned for Oprah at the start of the new school year, however, Vernita refused to let the

*Oprah and her father,
Vernon Winfrey, enjoy a
moment together. The strict
environment of her father's
home provided young Oprah
with the stability she needed
as a troubled teenager.*

child go with him. Vernita claimed that since she and Vernon had never been married, he had no parental rights. Unable to prove otherwise, Vernon had to leave Oprah with her mother. He has said, "I shed tears over having left her there, knowing that it wasn't the best environment for her."

It is not clear why Oprah's mother insisted that the child stay in Milwaukee with her. Because Vernita had to work very hard just to make ends meet, she had little time to spend with any of the children. Oprah was frequently left in the care of a 19-year-old cousin. One day, when she was only nine years old, her cousin raped her. The next day, he took her to the zoo, bought her an ice-cream cone, and told her that she had better not tell anyone what had happened.

Oprah did not really understand what had happened, but she blamed herself, thinking she had done something wrong. Her gift for being able to speak well failed her, and the "talkingest" child kept silent about the rape in the belief that her cousin's actions were her fault. The sexual abuse continued over the next five years, as her mother's boyfriend and an uncle also frequently molested the young girl.

Oprah has said that although the fear and shame were painful, the worst part of the experience was that others ignored what was happening. "There were people, certainly, around me who were aware of [the abuse]," she recalled, "but they did nothing." Like many child-abuse victims, Oprah began to act out. As often happens in such situations, she became promiscuous in her early teens. Years later Oprah would explain her behavior by saying that "not getting the attention from my mother made me seek it in other places, the wrong places."

At home Oprah became a rebellious teen, but at school she continued to be seriously interested in learning, determined to be a very good student. While the other students at Lincoln Middle School used the lunch hour to socialize, Oprah caught up on her reading. This solitary habit came to the attention of one of the teachers, Gene Abrams, who recommended that Oprah be admitted into Upward Bound, a program that sent promising minority students to better schools in the suburbs. Oprah was accepted into the program and soon afterward transferred to Nicolet High, a private school outside Milwaukee.

Very few African-American students attended the exclusive Nicolet High School. Most of Oprah's white classmates dismissed her as one of "the bus kids," because the black students had to ride a bus from their neighborhood to get to and from the school each day. But a few of the white students were civil and even friendly toward Oprah, inviting her to visit their homes.

It was hard for the young girl to see the disparities between the opulent lifestyles of her suburban white classmates and the meager existence her mother provided. Oprah wanted to have the same things other kids her age enjoyed. She also had pleasant memories of the simpler life she had known with her grandparents in Kosciusko. And she thought of the stable atmosphere she had enjoyed during the year she spent with her father and Zelma in Nashville. But the abuse that she so silently endured manifested itself in her behavior, and once again her mother began to believe that she could not handle Oprah.

In a desperate attempt to try to control her wayward daughter, Vernita Lee took the teenager to a home for wayward girls. Years later Oprah remembered the interview process: "They treat you like you're already a known convict." She also recalled thinking, "How in the world is this happening to me? I was 14 and I knew I was a smart person. I knew I wasn't a bad person, and I remember thinking: How did this happen? How did I get here?" In what may have been the most fortunate incident of her life, the girls' home had no space, and Oprah was sent home with her mother, who immediately called Vernon Winfrey for help. Vernon agreed that Oprah could come and live with him, and she returned to Nashville once again.

Oprah was 14 years old when she went to live with her father for a second time. She was full of secrets. She had never talked about male relatives and acquaintances sexually abusing her, and she also hadn't told anyone in

Nashville that she was pregnant. Vernon Winfrey later recalled, "We were [not] aware of her being pregnant when she came back until a week or two before she had the baby." Little is known about Oprah's pregnancy other than that she delivered a premature baby who died soon after birth. Oprah's half-sister, Patricia, sold the story to the *National Enquirer* in 1990, and Oprah's only public statement about the disclosure was to acknowledge that the story was true and that the experience was "the most emotional, confusing and traumatic of my young life."

Vernon Winfrey may not have known all the reasons his daughter was troubled, but he firmly believed that getting a good education was essential for her future success. He again provided her with the structure and discipline that he knew she needed, including enrolling her in school and establishing a strict curfew. Vernon encouraged Oprah to become active in church again and to participate in community service. He and Zelma made it clear that they expected Oprah to earn straight A's because she was a smart girl and was capable of making good grades. This came as a shock to the teenager, who had been settling for C's in Milwaukee. The Winfreys required Oprah to read extra books and learn 20 new words each week. Because of this reading, she became familiar with the writings of many African-American literary figures, such as Maya Angelou, and she had a better understanding of black culture than many of her African-American classmates.

The confused teenager once again thrived in the strict environment of her father's home, enjoying life more than she had in years.

In 1968, the city of Nashville, Tennessee, brimmed with opportunities for 14-year-old Oprah Winfrey as she began to put her troubled life back together.

3

GETTING IT TOGETHER

In the fall of 1968, Oprah Winfrey enrolled in East High School in Nashville—one of many newly desegregated schools at that time in the South. The class of 1971, of which she was a member, was only the second integrated class. East High was made up of approximately 70 percent white students. Unlike Oprah's experience at Nicolet High, at East High she was learning with students who were all generally from the same economic background. Oprah got along well with almost everyone, regardless of their race. Gary Holt, a white classmate and good friend, recalled that Oprah was "not white or black" and that "some of her black classmates would have said she was too white."

At school Oprah refused to dwell on issues of race, preferring to focus on problems that related to all students at her school. During her senior year she decided to run for president of the student government association. In her campaign, she talked about upgrading the cafeteria's food and having live music at the prom. Her slogan was "Vote for the Grand Ole Oprah," making a pun on her name, which closely resembled country music's most famous site, the

Grand Ole Opry, located in Nashville.

Holt believes that Oprah's religious beliefs contributed to her seeming to be almost color-blind regarding race. "She had enough influence from the Christian perspective to realize you can fight the injustice but it's the heart that has to change," he said in an interview. During the early 1970s, an awareness and an appreciation of black culture were rising to the forefront of African-American consciousness. Oprah, however, seemed unconcerned with such issues.

Active in many school events, Oprah represented East High School in 1970 at the White House Conference on Youth, held in Estes Park, Colorado. Sponsored by President Richard Nixon, the conference gathered young people and business leaders together to discuss issues that concerned teenagers. That year she was also selected to represent East High as an Outstanding Teenager of America.

It quickly became apparent that Oprah was an individual with something to say and somewhere to go. Public speaking grew to be a hobby for the enthusiastic student, and she joined the forensics team. She and other team members competed with other schools in debates sponsored by civic organizations.

That year Oprah went with a church group to give a recitation, or an oral interpretation, in Los Angeles. While there she visited the usual tourist spots, including Grauman's Chinese Theatre, where she saw the Walk of Stars, which honors famous film stars by displaying their names etched in concrete. Vernon Winfrey recalled that when his daughter came back from the trip she told him that one day her name would be on the Walk of Stars as well. Far from belittling her comments as a childish fantasy, he saw them as "the foreshadowing . . . that indeed she would one day be famous." Vernon remembered, "We knew she had great potential. We knew she had a gift and talent to act and speak when she was nine years old. She's never

President Richard M. Nixon sponsored the 1970 White House Conference on Youth, held in Estes Park, Colorado. Oprah joined other young people and business leaders there and participated in discussions about issues facing teenagers.

been a backseat person, in school or in church. She always loved the limelight."

Oprah, with all her drive and enthusiasm, soon opened the door to her future career. During her senior year, she wanted to help raise money for the March of Dimes by participating in a walkathon. In such events, sponsors donate a sum of money to a charity for every mile walked. Oprah needed to find corporate sponsors for the walkathon, so she approached WVOL, a local black radio station. She asked John Heidelberg, one of the station's disc jockeys, to contribute, and he agreed.

After the walkathon, Oprah returned to the radio

*When the teenage Oprah
first saw the Walk of Stars at
Grauman's Chinese Theatre
in Hollywood, California,
she decided that one day her
name would be there as well.*

station to collect the donation. While talking with the young fund-raiser, Heidelberg was impressed at how well she spoke and that she had no trace of a regional accent. After giving her the promised donation, he asked the teenager to tape a sample reading for him. Oprah made the recording, and when Heidelberg played it for the station general manager, Clarence Kilcrese, the executive was impressed by her delivery. "I needed part-timers at that time," Kilcrese later recalled. "I had two girls in mind, and I walked in and Oprah never stumbled one time. I said, 'This is the lady right here.'" He offered Oprah the job.

The high school senior was anxious to seize the opportunity, but she suspected her father would not be easy to convince. She was right. Vernon Winfrey was not sold on the idea. He was concerned that the job would interfere with Oprah's studies. But after his daughter persistently presented her case, he finally relented and allowed her to take the job under two conditions: she had to continue to go to school and the job had to remain part-time.

Soon Oprah fell into a routine. After school, she reported to the radio station, where she read news until 8:30 P.M. Then she went home and studied. She earned $100 a week—a great deal of money for a teenage girl during the early 1970s. She was also learning valuable skills. John Heidelberg took her under his wing and introduced her to the technical aspects of broadcasting.

Oprah kept up her grades, and she also remained involved with the forensics team. She was voted Most Popular Girl in her class in 1971 and dated the Most Popular Boy. Anthony Otey was an honor student like Oprah, and the two often met to rehearse her recitations for the forensics meets.

During her busy senior year, Oprah also started to enter and win beauty pageants. She had become popular among other employees at WVOL, and the station nominated her to compete in the 1971 Miss Fire Prevention beauty pageant. Oprah did well in the competition and became one of three finalists. Each finalist had to answer the same question: "What would you do with a million dollars?" After the other contestants had answered the judges, Oprah decided to go for humor and honesty. She replied, "I'd be a spending fool." Evidently her spontaneous candor charmed the judges because she won the competition, becoming the first black woman to win the Miss Fire Prevention title.

Oprah poses for her yearbook photo in 1971. Voted student government president and Most Popular Girl in her class, Oprah seized the opportunities presented to her and accomplished many remarkable things during her high school years.

The competition also may have reassured Oprah that she should trust her instincts. Years later she commented, "I had marvelous poise and talent and could handle any questions, and I would always win in the talent part, which was usually a dramatic reading. I could—I still can—hold my own easily. Ask me anything, and my policy has always been to be honest, to tell the truth. Don't try to think of something to say. Just say whatever is the truth."

In the few short years that she had been living with her father and stepmother in Nashville, Oprah Winfrey had turned her life around. The once uncontrollable young woman had become an excellent student, a forensics champion, a student government president, and the most popular girl in her class—and she had a solid job as a radio broadcaster.

Vernon was delighted with his daughter's progress and eager to see her enter college after graduation. Oprah had dreams of going to a school in another state so that she could have some distance between her strict father and herself, but he refused to let her leave town. Instead she enrolled at Tennessee State University (TSU), a large, African-American institution located right in Nashville.

The university did not offer a program in television and radio, the fields Oprah wanted to study, so she chose drama and speech as her majors. Her father wasn't happy with her choice, telling her, "I'm not sending you to school to become an actress."

Life at TSU exposed Oprah to more than the ideas of the classroom. The campus community reflected general trends going on across the country. A major issue with the student body was raising black consciousness. Although she knew of her black heritage and was proud of her black roots, Oprah did not share the views held by most of her classmates. Many were proponents of militant thinking who considered political demonstrations part of the college routine. Oprah stood apart from most of the student body.

"I refused to conform to the militant black thinking of the time. I hated, hated, hated college," she explained later in an interview, adding, "Now I bristle when someone comes up to me and says they went to Tennessee State University with me. Everybody was angry for four years. It was an all-black college and it was in to be angry. Whenever there was any conversation on race, I was on the other side, maybe because I never felt the kind of repression other black people are exposed to. I think I was called [a] nigger once, when I was in fifth grade."

Oprah's life on campus may not have been ideal or what she had hoped for, but she did well and impressed her professors. Dr. William Cox remembers her from his theater practice class. He said that they got along well because Oprah "knew what she wanted and where she was going." The young student threw herself into the university's drama department programs with great passion. In one performance she played Coretta Scott King, the wife of Martin Luther King Jr., in a drama written by another student. She also performed in several other school productions, while continuing to give dramatic recitals for church, stay on top of her studies and report regularly to her news broadcasting job at WVOL.

The college freshman also decided to continue competing in beauty pageants, in part because they could provide scholarship money to help pay for her education. In March 1972, she entered the Miss Black Nashville pageant, which was sponsored by the Negro Elks Club. While Oprah realized she was attractive, she knew that her real strength rested in

While a sophomore at Tennessee State University, Oprah became the first woman and the first African American to anchor the television news in Nashville.

the talent competition. She presented a dramatic reading and a song that, in the words of pageant director Gordon Brown, "knocked the audience off their feet." That performance earned her the title and qualified her for the Miss Black Tennessee pageant, to be held that June.

Six young women competed to become the first Miss Black Tennessee, and Oprah did not expect to win. She thought the judges would prefer one of her lighter-skinned competitors. To her amazement— and that of almost everyone else attending the competition—the judges declared Oprah Winfrey the 1972 Miss Black Tennessee. "I won on poise and talent," she later told a reporter. "I was raised to believe that the lighter your skin, the better you were. I wasn't light-skinned, so I decided to be the best and the smartest."

As the first Miss Black Tennessee, Oprah won a scholarship and an all-expense-paid trip to Hollywood, where she would compete in the Miss Black America pageant that August. The pageant itself was controversial. Many groups, including feminists and civil rights leaders, opposed the event, believing that beauty pageants were nothing more than opportunities to exploit young women. Some people later wondered if this controversy affected Oprah as she prepared for the event.

Dr. Janet Burch, a Nashville psychologist, accompanied Oprah to Los Angeles as her chaperone. Burch later noted that when she and Oprah went shopping to select the wardrobe required for the pageant, it appeared that "Oprah wanted to maximize her talent, her stability, her composure, her ability to answer questions. She completely minimized her physical attraction. That's just very unusual for a person who enters a beauty pageant."

As the pageant week progressed that August, Burch heard reports indicating that her young charge was receiving high marks from the judges. Some observers predicted that Miss Black Tennessee would win the contest. Oprah's voice was strong and compelling as she practiced singing the spiritual "Sometimes I Feel Like a Motherless Child" for the talent competition. She fit in well with the other young women during rehearsals for the program's opening act. Oprah and her chaperone spent evenings dining in fine restaurants and attending parties with celebrities.

Throughout the week, the contestants focused on

how the judges viewed their appearance and actions. "Oprah made good impressions because of the way she was able to conduct and handle herself," Dr. Burch observed. "She did not go off on tangents. She was very goal-oriented."

On the final night of competition, Oprah inexplicably decided not to wear the flattering costume she had chosen earlier, selecting instead a dowdy outfit. She also used little makeup and styled her hair in a very unsophisticated manner. Burch believed that Oprah was deliberately sabotaging her chances of winning the title.

Sure enough, Miss Black Tennessee did not win the crown. But afterward, when Burch found Oprah backstage, the young competitor showed no signs of being disappointed. Instead she seemed happy. Burch later told biographer Robert Waldron, "I had a sense it was almost a relief [for her not to win]. . . . Winning that pageant's like a hot potato. It was something she wanted, because it might help her career, but didn't want because she probably didn't want to play that role."

However, new opportunities soon presented themselves. Unbeknownst to Oprah, the affirmative action policies demanded by the political activists she had ignored on campus were about to work to her benefit. These policies increased the number of opportunities available to minorities and women for certain jobs and for acceptances to colleges and universities. During her sophomore year at TSU, the Federal Communications Commission (FCC) directed many television stations across the country to hire news staff members who belonged to minority groups. Nashville-based WTVF-TV, a CBS affiliate, was among the stations required to comply with the FCC order.

Members of the management team at WTVF-TV had already begun hunting for a minority person to fill an empty staff position when someone suggested interviewing Oprah. As an African American and a woman, she represented two minority groups. The fact that she also had the right qualifications and was a former beauty queen made her all the more appealing. WTVF was determined to have Oprah join its staff.

Oprah's warmth and self-assurance made her a natural in front of television cameras in Nashville, Tennessee, and established her as a young woman with great prospects.

4

THE TALK
OF THE TOWN

For someone eager to enter the communications field, Oprah was oddly reticent about going to WTVF. When the television station managers first phoned and expressed interest in interviewing her for a job, she put them off by explaining that she had to attend a biology class. Eventually she visited the station and was interviewed for the job by Chris Clark, the news director. Clark later said that the two things he remembered about Oprah were her poise and her tremendous self-assurance. He noticed what many other people would see in the years to come: Oprah was a natural in front of the camera.

Little did Clark know how Oprah truly felt. She recalled that before the interview, "I was such a nervous wreck, I had no idea what to do or say. And I thought . . . I'll just pretend I'm Barbara Walters [the popular ABC news anchor]. I will sit like Barbara, I will hold my head like Barbara. So I crossed my legs at the ankles, and I put my little finger under my chin, and I leaned across the desk, and I pretended to be Barbara Walters."

In 1973 Nashville was a laid-back town compared to major

Barbara Walters, shown here early in 1976 as the cohost of the NBC-TV Today *show, opened doors for women in the highly competitive television news market. Oprah recalls that when she interviewed for her first television job, she imitated the successful news anchor's mannerisms.*

cities such as Los Angeles and New York, according to Clark, and WTVF was looking for someone who would be neither too intimidating nor too casual. The station wanted to find someone who was like the "next door neighbor who knows what's going on and can tell you about it." In Oprah, Clark found exactly what he was seeking.

"You know, you look for people all the time," Clark has said, "and everybody you see on tape, there's always this nagging doubt. Well, she's okay, but her hair's not right. Her makeup's not right. Why didn't she dress better?" But Oprah's tape proved strikingly different. "It was unbelievable," he remembered. "You looked at Oprah the first time and you said, 'This is right. This will work.' It was just one of those things you don't experience very often."

WTVF offered Oprah a job as weekend news co-anchor. When the college sophomore received the news, the first thing she did was rush to her trusted professor, Dr. Cox. Oprah wanted his advice on whether she should give up school and radio to take the job at the television station. Cox told Oprah: "I've met some fools in my day. Don't you know that people go to college to get CBS to call them? Take it." He even gave her the dime to make the call. She took his advice and accepted the job. Although she had to quit her job at the radio station, she stayed in school, juggling her responsibilities at the television station with her college classes.

In 1973 Oprah started her job as WTVF's weekend news coanchor, which was news in itself. Not only was she the first woman Nashville had ever seen as a television news anchor, but she was also the first African American. Nobody knew how or if the public would accept Oprah. She was well aware that she had been hired as a "token" minority employee, but as she later put it, "I was a happy, paid token."

The station's concerns about how the public would respond to seeing a 19-year-old black woman on television quickly disappeared. "You've got to understand that this was the South," Clark later explained. "It was a very racially tense time in Nashville, and she was the first black woman on television. But there was not a complaint. People just accepted her."

Oprah and her coanchor, Harry Chapman, often

had to cover their own stories, write the scripts, and edit them before sitting down in front of the cameras to read the news. The new coanchor's debut before Nashville went smoothly enough, but Clark soon noticed that she got too involved with the work. "The problem with her was that she was just too people-oriented to be a hard-nosed reporter," he remembered. "If she went out and covered somebody's house burning down, instead of coming back and writing the story like a good reporter would, she would be working the phone lines trying to get them clothes, or help, or worrying about it, or worrying us about worrying about it. . . . It was just an extension of what she was at that very young age."

Everyone at WTVF could see that Oprah had special talents that would eventually take her far beyond Nashville. In the mid-1970s the field of television news was going through many changes. And the women working in broadcasting were making news themselves. The biggest story involved Barbara Walters, who in April 1976 was hired to coanchor the *ABC Evening News*, at a reported five-year salary of $5 million. In such an environment, Oprah could not ignore her own possibilities for advancement.

With Clark as her mentor, Oprah quickly went from being weekend news coanchor to weeknight coanchor. But it wasn't long before she was being scouted by stations with larger markets, including Baltimore television station WJZ, an ABC affiliate. Oprah knew that the viewing audience was much larger in Baltimore than in Nashville. In 1976, Baltimore claimed the 10th-largest market in the nation. She decided to move to Baltimore, where she would receive more exposure and a bigger salary. Oprah still needed to complete her senior class project to graduate, but she decided to finish earning her degree later.

A quirky ad campaign designed to create interest in WJZ's new anchor heralded Oprah's arrival in Baltimore.

"What's an Oprah?" was plastered on the sides of buses and billboards all over Baltimore. She was the first woman hired as an anchor. The station also wanted to draw attention to its extended evening news programming, which had been lengthened from 30 minutes to one full hour. WJZ executives were confident that their new employee would work well with coanchor Jerry Turner, a well-known figure in Baltimore who had been the evening news anchor since the late 1960s. They hoped that the new team would draw an even larger audience.

In spite of the excitement generated by Oprah's new position at WJZ, things did not go well once she arrived. Oprah had a hard time adjusting to the big city life of Baltimore, which was vastly different from

In the 1970s, Baltimore, Maryland, claimed the 10th-largest television market in the nation. In this city, Oprah discovered her strengths as a talk-show host, but often felt lonely being away from her family in Nashville.

Nashville. It was difficult not having her family around, and although she no longer had her father's curfew to abide by, she discovered that being on her own brought its own challenges. More than once, the 22-year-old woman called her family in tears.

"It took me a year to become charmed by Baltimore," Oprah once told a reporter. "The first time I saw the downtown area I got so depressed that I called my daddy in Nashville and burst into tears. In Nashville you had a yard even if you didn't have a porch. But the houses on Pennsylvania Avenue had neither."

From the start the executives at the station had tried to make Oprah feel welcome, even sending a dozen red roses with a note reading, "Please say yes," when they first offered her the job. However, after she came to the station, they didn't seem to know what to do with her. As the anchor for WJZ, she no longer exhibited her unique carefree style. Instead of coming across as spontaneous and relaxed, she seemed stiff and formal. Some people thought that Oprah was intimidated by her more experienced coanchor, Jerry Turner.

Before long everyone could see that the combination of Turner and Oprah wasn't working. Within nine months of being hired, Oprah was demoted to spot reporting. In a statement given to the *Baltimore Sun*'s television writer, WJZ said, "When people see how Oprah does on the assignments she is given, they will be convinced that the profile we have of Oprah is a high one." The station scrambled to rectify a situation that was starting to look like a fiasco.

To make matters worse, the station executives also told Oprah that she needed a makeover. Years later, in an interview with Mike Wallace, she remembered, "The assistant news director came to me and said, 'Your hair's too long. It's too thick. Your eyes are too far apart. Your nose is too wide. Your chin is too wide. And you need to do something about it.'" WJZ sent her to New York City and placed her in the care of what

Oprah described as "this chichi, pooh-pooh salon." The results were disastrous. "In a week I was bald," Oprah later recalled. "Just devastated. I had a French perm and it all fell out. Every little strand. I was left with three little squiggles in the front. They tried to change me, and then they're stuck with a bald, black anchorwoman. I went through a real period of self-discovery. You have to find other reasons for appreciating yourself. It's certainly not your looks."

The executives, still looking for solution, sent Oprah to a New York speech coach, who criticized her informal on-air manner as too friendly and urged her to toughen up. It seemed Oprah's bosses wanted everything about her changed.

The new spot reporter hated many of the assignments she was given. Threatened that she would be fired unless she complied, Oprah reluctantly interviewed a woman who had just lost her children and house in a fire. The station wanted Oprah to ask how the mother felt, but she believed it inappropriate to ask such a personal question so soon after a tragedy. After the interview, Oprah apologized to the grieving mother for intruding on her pain.

The struggling reporter had difficulty maintaining the required emotional distance from her stories. "You're at a plane crash," Oprah describes, giving an example, "and people are coming to find out if their relatives are in the crash and they're weeping, and you weep too because it's a tragic thing."

As dismal as her professional life seemed, Oprah developed some solid relationships in Baltimore. She found a lifelong friend in Gayle King Bumpas, who also worked at WJZ-TV. Oprah told *Redbook* that "one night there was this terrible snowstorm, so I invited Gayle, who was then living about 35 miles away, to stay at my house. She did—and we sat up and talked till dawn! Ever since then, we talk every day, sometimes three or four times." Oprah also became friends with one of the station's associate producers, Debra

Many people credit nine-time Emmy Award winner Phil Donahue, shown here on his program in 1985, with creating the daytime television talk-show format. Oprah Winfrey soon became his toughest competitor.

DiMaio, who in the future would be of great help to her professionally.

In the spring of 1977, WJZ-TV hired Bill Baker as its new general manager, and his innovative ideas soon helped the struggling reporter find her niche in television. Baker had been hired to help WJZ-TV compete against *Donahue,* an extremely popular, nationally syndicated talk show hosted by Phil Donahue. Baker wanted to develop a local program that would beat *Donahue* in the ratings. The new manager asked Oprah to think about being cohost of *People Are Talking,* a new show he was creating.

Having already been removed from the coanchor's desk, Oprah was understandably hesitant about accepting yet another career change. She worried that the position might prove to be another demotion, another step closer to being phased out of WJZ-TV entirely.

In spite of her concerns, she accepted the position. The station launched a huge promotional campaign and, to ensure a large audience for the program's debut, asked the cast of the daytime television drama *All My Children* to be the first guests. When *People Are Talking* debuted late in 1977, it was obvious that Oprah and cohost Richard Sher clicked. Oprah knew she had found her niche. "I came off the air, and I knew that was what I was supposed to do," she later said. "It just felt like breathing. It was the most natural process for me."

Executives at WJZ-TV knew they had a hit on their hands. Ratings began to skyrocket, and the show was soon beating all of the local competition. Soon afterward a disagreement between the station executives and Baker resulted in the hiring of a new general manager, Art Kern, who immediately saw that *People Are Talking* was "easily good enough to beat everything that was thrown against it by the local competition. We know [Oprah] was the margin of difference." Kern went on to say, "Richard was good—I don't mean to say he wasn't. But you could see that Oprah was the magic of the show."

Dick Maurice, entertainment editor of the *Las Vegas Sun* and a guest on the program, seconded Kern's assessment. Maurice remembered chatting with Oprah in the makeup room before one show. He started talking about his father and explained how the man had been injured in battle during World War II, leaving him with horrible scars on his face.

"I was telling her how kids would call me the son of Frankenstein," he recalled, "and how my father used to drop me off two blocks from school, rather than bear the embarrassment. . . . I looked over and tears were coming down [Oprah's] face. . . . She had a special quality about her that made her unique. There was this way she had of looking at you, and you felt that, when you were talking to her, the only person she was thinking about was you. It was a look in her eyes. You could see a soul there."

After hearing such good feedback, Kern approached Los Angeles-based Group W Production, the parent company of WJZ-TV, asking its executives to give *People Are Talking* a chance to break onto the national stage. Group W Production vetoed his idea. "She's pretty good," the executives said. "She'd appeal certainly in the major urban markets. But beyond that, we just don't think she has a future."

Years later, Kern looked back at Group W Production's decision and laughed. "[It] was probably one of the biggest mistakes ever made in television," he said. "I will tell you also that I didn't push hard enough for her. If I'd pushed harder as manager of the station, maybe we would have gotten something going beyond Baltimore. I take part of the credit for not discovering Oprah."

Professionally Oprah had at last come into her own, but on a personal level she was at her lowest. For four years she had been involved with a married man and was treated very badly in the relationship. Although friends had advised her to leave, Oprah had hung on. When the couple finally did break up, Oprah called in sick for three days. She began coping with the pain by overeating. On September 8, 1981, in a moment of desperation, Oprah penned a suicide note, instructing her friend Gayle King Bumpas to water her plants and to take care of her insurance papers.

"I don't think I was really serious about suicide," Oprah later said in an interview with *Ms.* magazine, "but I wrote my best friend a note. That suicide note has been much overplayed. I couldn't kill myself. I would be afraid that the minute I did it, something really good would happen and I'd miss it."

Whether serious or not, the contemplated suicide marked a pivotal moment in Oprah's life. Years later, after reading her journal entries from that time, she remarked that she "wept for the woman I used to be. I will never give my power to another person again." She came to realize how destructive the relationship had become and has said, "It was emotional abuse, which happens to women who stay in relationships that do not allow them to be all that they can be. You're not getting knocked around physically, but in terms of your ability to soar, your wings are clipped." She also began to recognize a pattern in her life: when she got depressed, discouraged, or stressed, she turned to food for comfort.

Oprah managed to pull herself from the depths of despair and take more control of her professional life. Through contacts she had made with stars from *All My Children*, the morning talk-show host landed a small role in the soap opera. The one-line part paid her only $183.75, but she hoped the appearance before a national audience might give her the exposure she needed to help further her career.

After six years in Baltimore, Oprah decided she would move on to a larger market. She considered several career possibilities. "I really grew up in Baltimore, you understand," she later explained. "I felt natural and cared for there. But it was time to move on. I made a deliberate choice where to go. Los Angeles? I'm black and female and they don't work in LA. Orientals and Hispanics are their minorities. New York? I don't like New York, period. Washington? There are thirteen women to every man in D.C. Forget it. I have enough problems."

Debra DiMaio, the former associate producer at WJZ-TV who had become one of Oprah's friends, played a decisive role in determining where the young television personality would move next. DiMaio had taken a job at WLS-TV in Chicago, working on that city's most popular talk show, *A.M. Chicago*. In 1983 the successful program had been plagued with difficulties. Within a week of the arrival of a new station manager and vice-president, the top news anchor had died and the host of *A.M. Chicago* had resigned. DiMaio knew that Oprah was thinking about making a change, so she asked her friend in Baltimore to submit an audition tape.

The tape created quite a stir. "That young woman was sensational," Dennis Swanson, the new station manager, later recalled. "I brought in all my program people, and they agreed. So I called her. When you've looked at as many audition tapes as I have, hers just jumped out of the stack." Adding to Oprah's appeal was the fact that she was beating *Donahue* in the ratings in Baltimore. Phil Donahue's highly rated talk show was based in Chicago, and Swanson wondered if Oprah could make *A.M. Chicago* a real threat to *Donahue*'s dominance in the local ratings.

Oprah agreed to come to Chicago for an interview. As part of the process, she had to do a trial taping of *A.M. Chicago*. Before making the tape, she had watched the 30-minute program from her hotel room and been unimpressed. Her own trial taping created quite a different reaction. After viewing Oprah at work, Swanson was ecstatic. He later described how "she came downstairs after the audition and wow, she said, how'd I do, and I said—I was trying not to be overly excited 'cause I still had to negotiate with her—and I said Oprah, that was fantastic."

Although Swanson seemed confident that Oprah was right for *A.M. Chicago,* Oprah herself wasn't so sure. She wanted to move on from Baltimore and advance her career, and she realized that hosting her own show would be a great opportunity. But she also remembered the fiasco that had followed her move to Baltimore. She didn't want WLS to try to change her the way the managers had tried at WJZ-TV. Discussing the situation with Swanson, she bluntly said, "You know I am black."

"Yeah, yeah, I'm aware of that," Swanson replied. "[B]ut Oprah let me tell you. I don't care what color you are. You can be green. All we want you to do is win. I'm in the business of winning and I want you to go for it."

Setting her misgivings aside, Oprah agreed to take the job at WLS-TV with a four-year contract and a salary reported to be $200,000 a year. After fulfilling her contractual obligations in Baltimore, she set off for Chicago, arriving just a few days before Christmas 1983. Lonely without her family and friends around her during the holidays, Oprah spent her first Christmas in Chicago working at a soup kitchen.

Isolated as she may have initially felt, Oprah soon embraced life in Chicago. Living there, she later said, "was like roots, like the motherland. I knew I belonged here." Just how perfect a match Oprah and Chicago made was about to be demonstrated in front of millions.

Oprah embraced life in Chicago after her move to the city in December 1983. "I knew I belonged here," she later said.

The Oprah Winfrey Show *established the popular talk-show host as a media force to be reckoned with.*

5

THE OPRAH WINFREY SHOW

On New Year's Day 1984, Oprah Winfrey started work in her new home as the host of *A.M. Chicago*. Viewers immediately took to the young woman and her spontaneous on-air manner. On *A.M. Chicago*, Oprah could choose any topic she wanted to discuss, and she brought her trademark candor to the show. In her first interview, with actor Tom Selleck, she caught him off guard by remarking on the color of his eyes. The new host also did other unexpected things such as kicking off her shoes and groaning, "My feet are killing me." People loved it.

The all-important ratings soon confirmed what everyone had already suspected. Within a month of Oprah's arrival, the size of the audience for *A.M. Chicago* had increased dramatically. Station manager Dennis Swanson noted that "there was no gradual build. She just took over the town." Many observers were stunned by Oprah's immediate success. Friends who had voiced doubts about her being able to make it on Phil Donahue's home turf sat back in wonder as her ratings continued to climb. "Everybody, with the exception of my best friend, told me that it wouldn't work," Oprah later recalled. "They said I was black, female, and overweight. They said Chicago is a racist city and the talk-show formula was on its way out."

Oprah's success continued. By early April, *A.M. Chicago* was regularly outdrawing *Donahue* in Phil Donahue's backyard. WLS executives were ecstatic.

Although Oprah's professional life in Chicago was starting off well, her personal life fared poorly. The loneliness she felt living in a new city caused her to fall back into her habit of overeating. Whenever she was under stress, which occurred more and more frequently, she went on monumental eating binges. Her tremendous success in turning around a failing talk show did nothing to ease the pressure, which instead increased as WLS executives moved quickly to expand the program to one hour. During her first six months in Chicago, Oprah gained 20 pounds. And people noticed. The more success her show achieved, the greater the size of the audience observing her appearance. "I'm overweight," Oprah admitted. "People tell me not to lose the weight; I might lose my personality. I tell them, 'Honey, it ain't in my thighs.'" While she might have publicly joked about the issue, Oprah was becoming very sensitive about any references to her weight.

The comments became more blunt. In December 1984, *Newsweek* ran a full-page article about Oprah's success in Chicago. While the talk-show host was thrilled by the publicity, she was extremely uncomfortable about the magazine's description of her as "nearly two hundred pounds of Mississippi-bred black womanhood, brassy, earthy, street smart and soulful."

Whatever her feelings about her weight may have been, Oprah continued to conduct herself professionally, making many public appearances and attending social functions for the television station. One of those functions was a farewell dinner in January 1985 for Phil Donahue. Donahue was moving his show from Chicago to New York City so that he could be closer

to his wife, actress Marlo Thomas, who worked in that city. At the event, Oprah joked that she was attending only to make sure Donahue left town, and Donahue quipped back that he wished her luck, "just not in my time slot!"

Beneath her jovial facade, Oprah was still concerned about what people were saying about her weight. As a result of the *Newsweek* article, Oprah was invited to appear on *The Tonight Show with Johnny Carson* in early 1985. Joan Rivers was scheduled to guest-host the show on the night Oprah would appear. Aware of some of the "fat" jokes the sharp-tongued comedian had made about actress Elizabeth Taylor, Oprah worried she was being set up for unkind comments about her own burgeoning weight. *Tonight* staffers assured Oprah that the show's focus would be on why *A.M. Chicago* was winning the ratings war against *Donahue*.

When the time came to tape the show, Oprah waited

Relaxing in her office in 1985, Oprah reflects on the success of both her television program and The Color Purple. *But at the same time, she was plagued by worries about her weight.*

nervously for her introduction. Suddenly she heard Joan Rivers saying, "I'm so anxious to meet her. They talk about her as streetwise, brassy, and soulful. Please help me welcome—Miss Oprah Winfrey." The audience broke into applause as Oprah crossed the stage to join Rivers. Soon the two women were discussing Oprah's life in Mississippi and her experiences as a beauty contestant. Then without warning, Rivers asked, "How did you gain the weight?"

Oprah replied, "I ate."

"You're a pretty girl and single," Rivers retorted. "Lose it."

The two women made a bet. Rivers would lose five pounds if Oprah lost 20. Oprah agreed to phone in weekly to report her progress and said that she would return to the show in March.

However, Oprah's plans to lose weight changed when she received the role of Sofia in Steven Spielberg's movie *The Color Purple,* but regardless her talk show continued to be a smash hit. After soundly beating *Donahue* in the ratings, the expanded *A.M. Chicago* was renamed *The Oprah Winfrey Show* and Oprah entered into discussions with WLS about syndicating the program nationally. While she had been able to negotiate an agreement to take time off for the filming of *The Color Purple,* she wanted to avoid similar situations in the future. If the show was syndicated, Oprah would have greater control over its programming and over her future career decisions. For its part, WLS would earn more money as part of its syndication deal with King World Productions than it would by continuing to keep *The Oprah Winfrey Show* a local program.

The WLS executives finally agreed, and as 1986 progressed, new partner King World Productions made plans to put the program in national syndication. The talk-show host and her syndication partner have never commented on the details of their arrangement, but the figures given in *Variety,* which specializes in the entertainment business, are astounding. *Variety* reported that the syndication deal gave Oprah a full 25 percent of gross sales of the show and projected that *The Oprah Winfrey Show* would gross $125 million in the first year and $150 million in the second year. According to the terms *Variety* reported, Oprah would receive just under $70 million during those two years.

While King World busied itself with preparing for the national release of *The Oprah Winfrey Show,* Oprah, with the help of her business manager—Jeffrey Jacobs—formed Harpo Productions. The company, named for Oprah—spelled backward—would oversee her future television and motion picture projects. Oprah also purchased an $800,000 condo in one of Chicago's best neighborhoods. She called the home a birthday present to herself for becoming a millionaire before she turned 32 years old.

At about the same time, Oprah caught the eye of Stedman Graham, a familiar figure within the Chicago social scene. A tall, slender, handsome man, Stedman worked for B&C Associates, a North Carolina public relations firm, and also modeled on the side. He had founded Athletes Against Drugs, a charity that arranges for sports figures to educate kids about the dangers of substance abuse.

Stedman had once asked Oprah out, but she had turned him down. Oprah was suspicious of his interest in someone who was both rich and overweight. Her staffers also suspected his motives and worried about her. "They figured if he looked like that, he either had to be a jerk or want something," Oprah said.

The two might never have connected if it hadn't been for the intervention of their friends. Suzanne Johnson, who runs a Chicago modeling agency, worked with some of Oprah's friends to plan a surprise appearance by Stedman on Oprah's show. He appeared, offering the stunned host a bunch of red roses, but

At first reluctant to date Stedman Graham, Oprah admits that his persistence eventually changed her mind. She describes her companion as "an overwhelmingly decent man."

even after that gesture Oprah turned down two more invitations from the persistent wooer.

When Stedman next asked Oprah for a date, she finally said yes. The two hit it off, and Oprah was soon describing him as "an overwhelmingly decent man. He has made me realize a lot of things that were missing in my life, like the sharing that goes on between two people."

Meanwhile, Oprah's professional success continued. On September 8, 1986, King World launched *The Oprah Winfrey Show* nationally, making her the first black woman to have a nationally syndicated talk show. Stephen W. Palley, senior vice president of King World, recalled, "The syndication of *The Oprah Winfrey Show* was a historic success, and a success of greater proportions than we had seen before. The show has huge household ratings and the kind of demographics advertisers like very much."

With so many other talk shows competing on the small screen, people wondered what made Oprah's so successful. Much of the credit goes to Oprah herself. She determined the show's format and subject matter. Debra DiMaio, who had been instrumental in bringing Oprah to Chicago, explained, "When Oprah got her own show, it was like bringing a child to an open schoolroom—you know, the open classroom, where you get to go crazy? Do whatever you want to do?" Oprah instinctively seemed to know what would work and what wouldn't. Some of her show topics were controversial, but she dealt with them all by using her guaranteed recipe for success: combining a mixture of candor, humor, and a natural ability to empathize with people. Oprah knew what viewers wanted and gave it to them.

Oprah was also a woman who knew what she wanted. When her show went national, she told the *Los Angeles Times* that she "wanted to be syndicated in every city known to man." She added that she did not expect much success going up against Donahue. "They say he's the king," she told the *Times*. "I just want a little piece of the kingdom." Actually, the popular talk-show host regularly took a sizeable segment of Donahue's audience.

Many viewers began to prefer Oprah's program to Phil Donahue's. Les Payne of *Newsday* wrote, "Oprah Winfrey is sharper than Donahue, wittier, more genuine and far better attuned to her audience, if not the world." Soon national ratings for *The Oprah Winfrey Show* rivaled the numbers for *Donahue*.

In February 1987 Oprah Winfrey and Phil Donahue

worked hard to create the better program, each hoping to claim the title of most-watched talk show during the all-important sweeps month. During sweeps months, which take place four times a year, ratings services find out how many people are watching each television program and what those people are like. Ad rates are determined from this information.

To help boost her ratings, Oprah decided to televise a program from Forsyth County, Georgia. Forsyth County had been in the news that year because the Reverend Hosea Williams, a civil rights leader, had led a march there to protest the county's 75-year-old practice of segregation. The county had been all white since 1912, when a white teenage girl claimed that three black males had raped her. The men were lynched for the alleged crime, and then every black person was forced out. No African Americans had lived there since.

During Williams's march, Ku Klux Klan supporters chanted racial slurs and held up inflammatory signs. The following week Williams return to Forsyth County, this time with more people, and the demonstration ended when 30 white protesters were arrested.

Oprah's decision to tape her show from Forsyth County created controversy, especially when she resolved not to include any African Americans in the audience. Always one to penetrate the heart of the issue, Oprah asked her all-white audience why Forsyth County had not allowed black people to live there for 75 years. One member of the audience replied, "[Blacks] have a right to live wherever they want to. But we have a right to have a white community, too." Oprah observed, "I like the way you speak of them. It's like, you know, black people come from Mars or something."

When it aired, the program earned almost double the ratings of Donahue's show. By March 1987, *The*

Oprah Winfrey Show was consistently beating *Donahue* in the ratings.

People in the industry began to recognize Oprah's amazing success. In 1987, she became the youngest recipient of the prestigious Broadcaster of the Year Award, given by the International Radio and Television Society. Later that year, Oprah was asked to be the first woman to host the Daytime Emmy Awards. She also received her first Emmy as Outstanding Talk/Service Show Host. *The Oprah Winfrey Show* itself received Emmy Awards for Outstanding Talk/Service Show and Outstanding Direction of a Talk/Service Show.

Oprah insists on discussing tough issues on her show. Here, during a broadcast in 1988, she engages the audience in a discussion on school violence.

Oprah was the darling of talk television, but not everyone admired her style. In a 1987 article, the *Saturday Evening Post* reported that some black viewers thought that her "touchy-feely" manner toward her mostly white audiences was too much like that of the stereotypical Southern mammy. In a 1988 *People* magazine article, writer Jeff Jarvis attacked the topics discussed on *The Oprah Winfrey Show*, listing his "Top-10 favorites" from the previous week, which included Hairdresser Horror Stories; Housewife Prostitutes; Men Who Fight over Women; Man-Stealing Relatives; Polygamy; Sexy Dressing; Get Rich and Quit Work; and Women Who Are Allergic to Their Husbands.

Oprah stolidly defended her show's programming. "I live my life and I do this show to try to raise people's consciousness," she explained, "to give people a sense of hope in their lives. So when people write or say negative things about me it really upsets me, because it means they don't understand me or what my show is about. They've missed it."

Oprah chose 1987 as the year to deal with some unfinished business. Her father had always placed great emphasis on the importance of getting an education, and he never let her forget that she had not earned her college degree. To put the matter to rest, Oprah re-enrolled in TSU and completed her senior project. She not only received her diploma but also delivered the commencement address. Vernon Winfrey watched his daughter repeat his own words to the full house: "You need that degree." Oprah then announced that she was endowing 10 scholarships to the university in her father's name.

Although often generous toward others, Oprah also spent her hard-earned money on herself. When someone asked her about her ostentatious lifestyle, she responded, "It's hard for me to remember drawing water from the well every morning and playing with corncob dolls." Surrounded by luxuries, she still didn't

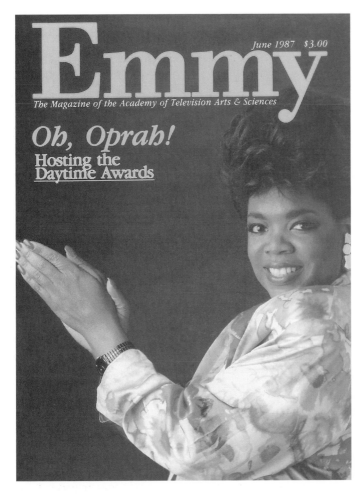

Emmy

June 1987 $3.00

The Magazine of the Academy of Television Arts & Sciences

Oh, Oprah!
Hosting the
Daytime Awards

In 1987, Oprah became the first woman to host the Daytime Emmy Awards. The previous year she had won the first of what would be many Emmy Awards for Outstanding Talk/Service Show Host

think of herself as a celebrity. In a 1987 interview with the *Saturday Evening Post,* she revealed, "This morning, as I sat in my marble tub, surrounded by bubbles, with the water pouring from a golden swan faucet, I thought, as I opened my box of apple-cinnamon soap, 'Is this it? Is this what being a celebrity is all about?' It's interesting because I don't feel any different. My ability to acquire things has changed, but I don't feel any different. So, I keep saying to myself. 'Well, I guess I'm not a star yet, because I don't feel like one.'"

Opulent as her lifestyle may have appeared to others, the woman who grew up on a small farm and

Eleven years after leaving Tennessee State University, Oprah returned to complete her degree requirements and deliver the commencement address.

experienced the tough streets of Milwaukee was not about to fritter her money away. In another interview given in 1987, she stated, "I have allotted myself to personally only spend a million dollars this year. That's how much I'm giving myself to play with. I can do that without worrying if this ends, will I have enough to eat."

In the following year, Oprah purchased a building in Chicago to house Harpo Production Studios. The building was renovated and transformed into a $20 million complex for use in taping *The Oprah Winfrey Show,* as well as other film and television projects. The structure contains two large studios, a darkroom, a carpentry and painting workshop, a kitchen, conference rooms, and offices for 150 staff members.

Harpo Productions allowed Oprah to do what she did best: address controversial and volatile issues in a way that she believed would help people improve their lives. She could show viewers that she was no stranger to dealing with trouble and that she was not afraid to admit to it. As part of this honest approach, Oprah began to address the issue of her weight publicly. The topic seemed to be of as much concern to her fans as it was to the host herself.

In July 1988 Oprah began using a liquid diet. That November she highlighted the results of the diet by coming onstage wearing a pair of size 10 Calvin Klein jeans and pulling a wagon loaded with 67 pounds of animal fat—the exact amount of weight she had lost. When asked by fans if she would gain the weight back, she replied, "I've been there—and I don't intend to go back."

During the following year, however, more stress sabotaged Oprah's commitment to stay slim. In March, problems with her extended family grabbed the attention of national newspapers and magazines. Articles described how her half-brother, Jeffrey, who had developed AIDS, felt abandoned by his family, including his half-sister. Oprah's defenders pointed out that although she had never been close to Jeffrey since she had moved away from her mother's home in Milwaukee at age 14 (Jeffrey was six at the time), she still provided her half-brother with financial support through their mother. Follow-up news items described how Vernita spent the money on herself and had even

Standing before her November 15, 1988, studio audience Oprah shows off her size-10 blue jeans and exults over her 67-pound weight loss.

given Jeffrey's landlord a bad check, causing Jeffrey to be evicted.

That same month, *The Women of Brewster Place,* the first movie created by Harpo Productions, aired on national television. Oprah both starred in and produced the movie. Like *The Color Purple, The Women of Brewster Place* generated complaints of black male bashing, but it also drew huge ratings and prompted ABC to contract with Harpo Productions for 13 episodes of a spin-off television drama series.

The Oprah Winfrey Show remained popular, but its talk-show format began to come under increasing criticism for exploiting people's tragedies and focusing on cheap, vulgar topics. Ignoring her critics, Oprah continued choosing subjects for her show that she believed would enlighten and assist her viewers in dealing with their problems. The controversy only added to the many ordeals of 1989.

During that summer and fall, Oprah also tried to help her nieces, whose mother, Patricia Lee, had substance-abuse problems and was reportedly leaving them alone for days at a time. In October of that year, Oprah's half-sister asked the celebrity for help with her drug problem, and Oprah enrolled her in a rehabilitation program.

Then, just three days before Christmas, Jeffrey Lee died from AIDS. "For the last two years," Oprah commented in a formal statement, "my brother, Jeffrey Lee, had been living with AIDS. My family, like thousands of others throughout the world, grieve not just for the death of one young man, but for the many unfulfilled dreams and accomplishments that society has been denied because of AIDS."

With the new year, Oprah focused her energies on the Harpo Productions new television series *Brewster Place.* The series debuted on May 1, 1990. Critics harshly criticized the show, calling it bland, and after only four episodes, the program was cancelled. Oprah

Oprah starred as Mattie Michael in The Women of Brewster Place, *a television movie that drew huge ratings. The first film created by Harpo Productions, its success prompted ABC to contract for a spin-off television series.*

was disappointed, but ABC still had plans for Harpo Productions and the nation's most popular talk-show host. Later that month, the television network announced that Harpo would produce four television movies, with Oprah starring in two of them.

Oprah was excited about her growing relationship with ABC, but her weight continued to be a concern. During the two years since her widely publicized weight loss, she had regained every pound—in part because of the ongoing pressure she had faced. Ready to deal with her problem openly again, she presented a segment on her show called "The Pain of Regain." Oprah told viewers that "if you lose weight on a diet, sooner or later you will gain it back."

Like many dieters, Oprah had struggled with a yo-yo dieting syndrome. Losing and gaining weight in the public eye made it all the harder. "I remember thinking why can't I control this," she once admitted. "I can control everything else in my life. I truly understand the frustration of it all. We [overweight people] are as intelligent and fun and charming and likeable as anybody else in the world. But you feel so badly about yourself because you have this monkey on your back."

It wasn't until late 1991 that Oprah finally began to understand the root causes of her weight problem. She declared insightfully in an interview with *People* magazine:

> My greatest failure was in believing that the weight issue was just about weight. It's not. It's about not being able to say no. It's about not handling stress properly. It's about sexual abuse. It's about all the things that cause people to become alcoholics and drug addicts.

Soon she would recognize the truth of those words and make changes in her own life.

In November 1991 Oprah testified at a hearing before the Senate Judiciary Committee, where she supported legislation requiring background checks on child-care workers. Such laws could reduce child abuse, one of many tough issues Oprah brought to national attention.

6

CONFRONTING TOUGH ISSUES

Underlying Oprah's struggles with weight were larger issues, issues she often took up on her television show. In one program Oprah revealed her personal history of sexual abuse for the first time. Her public-relations people had advised her that a public admission of this fact might tarnish her image. But keeping the abuse a secret had continued to make Oprah believe that something she'd done had caused the abuse. Realizing that this was a perception she shared with many other victims of abuse, Oprah made sure that her show presented abused people as the victims of crime, not the causes of it. "The truth is the child is never to blame," said Oprah in a 1991 interview. "It took me 37 years to figure that out."

Oprah was so concerned about the issue of sexual abuse that she began a national campaign in 1991 to educate people to help prevent it. The talk-show host had been donating money to child advocacy groups for many years and had on occasion used her program to draw attention to the appalling rise in crimes against children in the United States. Another reason she was moved to launch her national campaign was in reaction to a piece on the evening news about Angelica Mena, a young Chicago girl who was molested and murdered and then thrown into Lake Michigan. Angelica's confessed murderer had previously been convicted of two other abuse crimes. Oprah said that when she learned of the crime she "vowed that night to do something, to take a stand for the children of the country."

Oprah hired former Illinois governor James Thompson, a partner in the Chicago law firm of Winston and Strawn, to draft a federal child protection law that would create a data bank of convicted offenders of child abuse and other serious crimes. "When millions of people look at you to both set an example and to add your voice to theirs," Thompson said of his client, "it empowers you to do more than you ordinarily might. This is a woman with extraordinary commitment." Oprah also used her considerable fame to get Senator Joseph Biden, chairman of the Senate Judiciary Committee, to sponsor her proposal.

By this point in her career, Oprah had earned enough credibility to be invited to testify before the Senate Judiciary Committee. "I wept for Angelica," Oprah told the senators, "and I wept for us, a society that apparently cares so little about its children that we would allow a man with two previous convictions for kidnaping and rape of children to go free after serving only 7 years of a 15 year sentence."

The bill that Oprah hoped to get passed provided funding for an FBI database that would allow schools and other agencies that care for children to check the backgrounds of present and future employees. Senator Biden stated that the bill was "the best proposal to come before us. The idea is simple: that you must do everything you can to detect the convicted criminal before . . . another tragedy takes place." Soon dubbed "the Oprah Winfrey Law," the proposed legislation gained support from a number of representatives and senators. However, it failed to become law that year in part because it was attached to a larger crime bill that was vigorously opposed by the National Rifle Association and other interest

groups. Dismayed at the bill's failure, Oprah was not encouraged that the law *almost* passed. "Almost," she said, "doesn't save a child."

Oprah continued to receive recognition for her work to improve the lives of other people. In 1991 she attended a dinner emceed by famed actor and comedian Bill Cosby. The event honored Oprah and journalist Irv Kupcinet as winners of the Humanitarian Award, given by the Jesse Owens Foundation. Oprah was recognized for her $1 million gift to Morehouse College in Atlanta, Georgia, a historic African-American school for men.

As 1992 began, Oprah continued to experience professional success. One highlight in her television career that year was the prime-time interview conducted with pop singer Michael Jackson on February 10. The international star had not been interviewed for 14 years, and both his fans and critics were thrilled

Oprah's 1992 televised interview with Michael Jackson marked the first interview given by the pop singer in 14 years. About 90 million people watched at least part of the show.

at the opportunity to see the star once more on screen. An astonishing 39.3 percent of U.S. homes watched the program, and about 90 million people saw at least part of the show.

The Oprah Winfrey Show continued to maintain its number one position in its time period, and in June Oprah received her third Emmy Award as Outstanding Talk Show Host. But as Oprah stood to accept her Emmy Award that year, knowing that she weighed 237 pounds, she decided it was time to try to conquer her weight problem again. That summer she spent three weeks at the Doral Hotel, a spa in Telluride, Colorado. While there she met the spa's exercise physiologist, Bob Greene. This encounter marked a turning point in her struggles with her weight.

Greene knew very little about Oprah Winfrey when he first met her, but he knew how to deal with fitness issues. He has said that, like most people, Oprah wanted a quick fix, a secret formula. But his approach to weight control is holistic, dealing with the whole person rather than simply focusing on diet and losing weight. In his first session with Oprah, Greene evaluated her fitness level. Then he asked, "How often do you experience real joy?" Oprah confessed her initial confusion at the question: "It just threw me. Joy!? Who has time for joy?" But the conversation got her thinking about her life in new ways.

That fall, Oprah plunged into an incredibly busy schedule. She continued shooting her daily television program, and she announced her engagement to Stedman Graham, news that drew national attention. As part of her ongoing efforts to address the issue of child abuse, Oprah also hosted the television documentary "Scared Silent: Exposing Child Abuse." The hour-long show aired on CBS, ABC, NBC, and PBS in September. It marked the first time in television history that a non-news event was aired during prime-time by all major networks.

As host of the documentary, Oprah introduced the topic: "I'm Oprah Winfrey and like millions of other Americans, I'm a survivor of child abuse. I was only nine years old when I was raped by my 19-year-old cousin. He was the first of three family members to sexually molest me." Making child molestation a personal issue was an effective way to spotlight the problem. Oprah hoped that the broadcast would empower "children and adult children everywhere so they know they do not have to stand alone. It's time to stop the pain and suffering of children, and make the world a safer place for all of us."

Arnold Shapiro, the film's producer, said that making the film helped him realize the insidious nature of child abuse. "The undeniable reality," he explained, "is that all of us are victims of child abuse because we all pay the price in dealing with victims who act out their rage and hurt on society. What begins as a family crisis becomes society's burden, expense and responsibility."

Oprah hoped that the documentary would help get the child protection bill through Congress. The tactic seemed to work. In 1993, both houses of Congress passed the National Child Protection Act, and President Bill Clinton later signed it into law. Oprah and many other people who had fought for the bill's passage were present to witness the historic event.

Oprah also continued to be a voice for relevant issues when she starred in the 1993 television movie *There Are No Children Here*. The film deals with the struggles of a single mother raising her two sons in the Henry Horner Homes, one of Chicago's public housing projects. Oprah explained, "You find people in the projects who have as much desire for fulfillment and enrichment—to be somebody—as anywhere else in the world." She donated her salary from filming the movie to a newly formed scholarship fund for local children, and she started Families for a Better Life. The goal of the non-profit foundation was to help 100 families

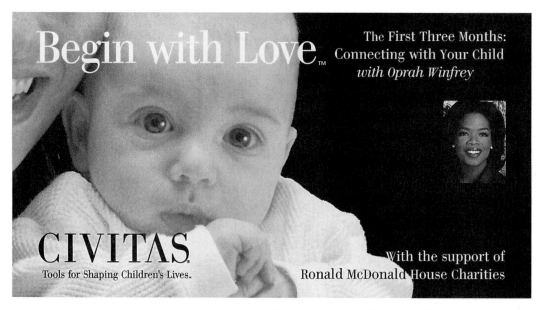

Begin with Love. ™

The First Three Months:
Connecting with Your Child
with Oprah Winfrey

CIVITAS.
Tools for Shaping Children's Lives.

With the support of
Ronald McDonald House Charities

Oprah's concern for children motivates her to contribute time and money to many projects designed to improve their lives, including this video for new parents, which she narrated.

move out of the projects by subsidizing them with $30,000 a year. Although ultimately the program was not successful, Oprah continued to donate large amounts of money to various organizations designed to help people better their lives.

For Oprah, 1993 was a year of successes and failures. That year she received the Horatio Alger Award from the Horatio Alger Association of Distinguished Americans, "given to those who overcome adversity to become leaders in their field." Proceeds from the awards dinner helped to raise money for college scholarships.

Oprah began working with Joan Barthel to write her autobiography, which was scheduled for release in September. Then, suddenly the publication date of the book was postponed, which caused rumors to circulate. Some people said that Oprah's family and fiancé, shocked by the book's frankness about her sexual activity during her teen years, convinced her to postpone the release. In an interview with *Ebony* magazine, Oprah simply stated, "I wanted to write a book that would empower people. A book that would connect the dots of my life in such a way as to give it meaning and in the process offer some sense of wisdom for other people in their lives. But I didn't have the clarity or the insight yet where I thought I could do that." In a press release about the book Oprah added, "I am in the heart of a learning curve. I feel there are important discoveries yet to be made."

It wasn't until four years later that Oprah revealed in an interview that one of the major reasons she did not release the book was her weight. "I was 227 lbs. when I was writing that autobiography," she said, adding later, "It would have been a disservice to me and to everyone else to write a book in that state of being. Being a food addict, literally, and not having control of your life is no position to be talking about yourself."

But Oprah was also working to do something once and for all about her weight and the issues related to it. She was determined that, by 1994, she would be ready to celebrate her 40th birthday with a lean, strong body. To help her get in better shape, she brought in Bob Greene, the exercise physiologist she had met in Colorado the previous summer. Their first workout together in Chicago took place on March 15, 1993. Greene started by telling Oprah his conditions for working with her: "I'm only going to work with you if you're willing to be here every day without fail, no excuses. You have to put in at least 40 minutes. And, on a scale from one to ten, you'll need to work at a level seven." Oprah agreed.

The exercise routine, combined with modified eating habits, produced a slow but steady weight loss. More importantly, the program made Oprah feel good. She began to have some of those moments of joy that Greene had asked her about when they'd first met. Oprah's hard work paid off. Later in 1993 she successfully completed a half-marathon, running roughly 13 miles, and by November she had reached her goal weight of 150 pounds.

Oprah knew that she would greet her 40th birthday in

better shape than she had been in for decades. So she set a new goal for herself. She told Greene that at some point during 1994, she wanted to run a marathon, a race of 26 miles and 385 yards. The two agreed on aiming for the Marine Corps Marathon, scheduled to take place in Washington, D.C., in October 1994. Determined to succeed, Oprah ran 10 to 12 miles every weekday morning before taping her shows. Then she would go on longer runs of 15 or 20 miles on the weekends.

When race day arrived, rain poured from the skies. Refusing to be discouraged, Oprah began her run. As the miles passed, she became more confident, and after she succeeded in running through the pain of the 21st mile, she knew she would finish the race. Oprah completed the marathon in just under 4 hours and 30 minutes, the time she had set as her goal for finishing the race. She could claim it as a huge personal victory.

Amby Burfoot, the editor of *Runner's World,* followed Oprah's progress throughout the marathon. He was so impressed with her perseverance that he put Oprah on the cover of his magazine the following spring. "She has made me a believer," Burfoot said. "More than that, in fact, I guess you could say I've been inspired."

Bob Greene agreed. "People will say to me, 'Oprah's got it easy because she has a personal chef and a personal trainer,'" he said. "But that's baloney. No one can run for you. She was on the track every morning. She worked herself as hard as any athlete I've seen. She deserved the results she achieved."

During 1994, Oprah also was inducted into the Academy of Television Arts and Sciences Hall of Fame. She had initially declined to accept the honor, claiming that others had contributed more to television than she had. "I wrote them back and told them, 'I think you have the wrong girl.' It just blows me away," she admitted. The American television personality was also honored overseas by the British Academy of Film and Television Arts, which gave her its award for best foreign television program.

Oprah participates in the 1997 Revlon Run/Walk for Breast Cancer fund-raiser. She worked out daily with her personal trainer, Bob Greene, changed her diet, and ran more than 10 miles every day. Oprah's discipline and hard work paid off and she reached her goal of developing a lean, strong body.

Not everyone was a fan, however. In 1994 Oprah became embroiled in staff problems. Her former employee Colleen Raleigh sued the talk-show host. Raleigh, who had worked for *The Oprah Winfrey Show* as senior publicist for eight years, stated that she "could no longer work in an environment of dishonesty and chaos." Claiming that she could not "foster the image of Oprah Winfrey, *The Oprah Winfrey Show* and Harpo as happy, harmonious and humane," Raleigh filed suit against Oprah, seeking more than $200,000 in salary, bonuses, and severance pay she claimed was due her. The case was settled out of court for an undisclosed amount.

At about the same time, Oprah's friend Debra DiMaio, who had been instrumental in bringing the talk-show host to *A.M. Chicago* back in 1984, was also experiencing a storm of criticism from other employees and left the company. DiMaio reportedly received a severance package worth $3 million.

Perhaps these conflicts led Oprah to a period of deep reflection during which she decided that her show needed changes. In a 1994 interview with *Entertainment Weekly,* she admitted, "I've been guilty of doing trash TV and not even thinking it was trash. I don't want to do it anymore. But for the past four years we've been leading the way for doing issues that change people's lives. So I'm irritated and frustrated at being lumped in with those other shows."

The following year, Oprah took an even firmer stand against what has been called "sleaze TV." She made concentrated efforts to distance herself and her show's format from programs such as *Geraldo* and *Ricki Lake,* choosing to focus on personal growth and other important issues, rather than on titillating scandal. "We've grown in the past ten years, the audience, the show and I," she explained in an interview in 1995. "And I want the shows to reflect that growth— even if our ratings go in the tank."

Oprah's warning about declining ratings proved to be prophetic. While the show remained number one, its lead over its nearest competitors shrank considerably. Oprah was more concerned over how the program was viewed, however, and its new philosophy gained her more credibility and respect from former detractors.

With the changes, one thing remained constant: Oprah was determined to be honest. How open she was willing to be became clear on a program about women who used drugs. It aired January 13, 1995. During the show, Oprah said to one of the guests, "I did your drug." Oprah went on to tearfully explain that she had been involved with a drug user and that she had used illegal drugs when she was with him. When he was gone, the talk-show host continued, the drugs were gone. One of the guests, a *Washington Post* reporter, spoke with Oprah after the show and said that Oprah told her that she would have "felt like a hypocrite" if she had not mentioned her drug use.

As she admitted her own mistakes, Oprah remained committed to helping young women in similar difficult situations find a way out. She continued to believe that one part of the solution was education. In 1995, Oprah donated $1 million to Atlanta's Spelman College, a historically African-American women's school. The successful talk-show host wanted to help women establish careers in the sciences and mathematics, and she specifically designated that her donation was for helping science faculty and students conduct research in environmental biology, atomic physics, and synthetic chemistry. "I am delighted to be part of the extraordinary legacy of Spelman College and Dr. Johnnetta Cole [president of Spelman], whose vision has empowered thousands of young African American women," she said. "This Science Initiative is a gift to us all, as it allows the next generation to discover new ways to really make our world better."

The year was not without personal problems, however. Oprah's father became involved in a lawsuit at Tennessee State University, where he was the administrator of the 10 scholarships funded by Oprah. In a handwritten affidavit, Pamela Kennedy, a 28-year-old junior, claimed that when she went to Vernon Winfrey for advice about scholarship money, he made sexual advances toward her. Kennedy filed a $3 million law-suit. Vernon Winfrey denied the accusation and said that he believed the charges were made in an attempt to get some of his daughter's money. In a press statement Oprah said, "I am appalled that his reputation is on the line because of an unsubstantiated accusation." The charges were dropped when an investigation of the woman's claims did not produce sufficient evidence to pursue the case.

Throughout 1995, Oprah continued to press for excellence on her television program, apparently unconcerned with the show's ratings. Her zeal was rewarded in 1996 when she won the prestigious George Foster Peabody Individual Achievement Award. Described as the "Olympics of the broadcast and cable industry," the Peabody Award is the media industry's most coveted prize. After attending a ceremony to accept the honor, Oprah immediately advised everyone, "You should be getting home because the Oprah show is on right now."

Later that year, the talk-show host decided to promote education and reading on her program by forming an on-air book club. Despite skepticism from others, she went ahead with the plan of having a monthly show devoted to the discussion of a novel of her choosing. Oprah's Book Club started a revolution in the book publishing industry, and previously obscure books that were named as Oprah selections regularly ended up on best-seller lists.

Oprah's own work was appearing on best-seller lists as well. Because she had been so successful in losing weight and becoming fit with Bob Greene's help, the two collaborated to write *Make the Connection: Ten Steps to a Better Body and a Better Life,* which was published in the fall of 1996. A year later, a companion video that Oprah produced was also released. Proceeds from sales of the video were donated to a Boston-based program called A Better Chance (ABC). ABC recruits

minority students who have neither the resources nor the advantages to gain admittance to college, and the program provides them with a quality education. Oprah took pride in her involvement with ABC and the fact that more than 90 percent of the students enrolled in it later went on to college.

But 1996 also set the stage for a major legal battle. Early that year, on April 16, Oprah aired a show that included a segment on food quality. The British government had determined that people in the United Kingdom were dying in growing numbers from mad cow disease, called new variant Creutzfeldt-Jakob disease when it appears in humans. The scientist who headed the British research committee said that millions of

In 1996 Oprah decided to devote one television program a month to an on-air book club. Writers such as Toni Morrison (left) saw their books catapult to the top of best-seller lists after appearing on Oprah's Book Club list.

people could be carrying the disease without knowing it because the condition is undetectable when first contracted. Years or even decades could pass before an infected person showed any symptoms.

Oprah's guest on the show was Howard Lyman, a director of the Humane Society of the United States. Lyman stated that U.S. cattle were being fed beef protein, even though the federal government had banned this practice because of the possibility that the animal protein might carry the disease. He believed the practice could cause an epidemic that would "make AIDS look like the common cold." After hearing what Lyman had to say, Oprah asked her audience, "Now doesn't that concern you all a little bit, right here, hearing that? It has just stopped me cold from eating another burger."

Not only did Oprah stop eating beef, so did many other Americans. Beef prices plummeted nationwide in what some called the "Oprah Crash of 1996." In 1997, Texas ranchers headed by Paul Engler sued Oprah, claiming that the show's "carefully and maliciously edited statements were designed to hype ratings at the expense of the American cattle industry." The suit went to trial under a Texas statute called the False Disparagement of Perishable Food Products Act. Under this statute, lawsuits could be filed against people who falsely criticized the value of fruits, vegetables, or meats.

Paul Engler claimed that he lost $6.7 million when the beef prices dropped for a full two weeks after Oprah's show had aired. But he had to convince the court that what Oprah had said on her show was false. Oprah and her lawyers countered by claiming that food disparagement laws are an infringement of America's First Amendment, which guarantees the right to free speech. The court ruled that live cattle are not perishable food products, but it allowed the court action to continue as a business disparagement suit. The trial began in Texas on January 21, 1998.

Oprah leaves the federal courthouse in Amarillo, Texas, in January 1998. After hearing about five weeks of testimony in a business disparagement suit brought against Oprah by Texas ranchers, jurors decided the case in Oprah's favor.

Never one to miss an opportunity, Oprah taped a series of shows from Amarillo, Texas, where the trial took place. Her programs showcased various aspects of Texas life, including mansions, big hairdos, multimillionaire bachelors, and celebrities such as country singer Clint Black and actor Patrick Swayze. The trial lasted five weeks, and in the end Oprah won. Exiting the courthouse after the judge declared she was "not liable for any damages to the Texas beef industry," Oprah proclaimed, "Free speech not only lives, it rocks." Her shows from Texas brought extremely high ratings, and Oprah felt that at last she was successfully separating her program from "sleaze TV."

Successful ventures during 1998, including the popular television miniseries The Wedding, *which starred Halle Berry (left), proved that Oprah was at the top of her game.*

7

AT THE TOP
OF HER GAME

More triumphs for Oprah followed in 1998. In February a two-part, four-hour miniseries named *The Wedding* aired on ABC. Based on a novel by African-American writer Dorothy West, the program was the second in a series of six television movies to be produced under the banner of *Oprah Winfrey Presents*. West's novel drew on her experiences as a longtime resident of Oak Bluff, the exclusively black community within the larger town of Martha's Vineyard, Massachusetts.

The Wedding takes place during the 1950s and focuses on Shelby Coles, played by Halle Berry. Shelby is the mixed-race daughter of one of the wealthy Vineyard families. The matriarch of the family, Gram, is white—the daughter of a former slave owner. During the post-Civil War era, Gram reluctantly allowed Shelby's mother, Corinne, to marry a black man to ensure that the family's lineage would continue. However the older woman was determined that her family would become lighter-skinned with every succeeding generation.

However, Shelby's romance with Lute McNeil, a white jazz

Many cast members of The Wedding *(above) agreed to participate in the project because it explored an aspect of African-American life overlooked by many Americans.*

musician who has been married three times before and is suspected to be a wife batterer, is not what Corinne had in mind for her daughter. Only Shelby's grandmother approves the marriage, and clearly it is in large part because the groom is white.

Like many of her projects, *The Wedding* intrigued Oprah because it explored part of African-American life that was largely unrecognized by most of America. In a message sent to television critics before the show's release, Oprah said, "It's a really important miniseries . . . [because] it reveals a world that's unfamiliar to most people, a world where there are highly educated, wealthy, successful black families on Martha's Vineyard, in the early 1950's. But it [also] explores themes related to everybody, regardless of your race or background—the bonds of family, the legacies and values that we pass on to each other, whether those are right or wrong."

Other cast members were also drawn to the story because of its subject matter. Halle Berry had not read *The Wedding* when Oprah first asked her to play the role of Shelby. The young actress had no idea that African Americans like the characters described in the book lived in Martha's Vineyard. The story appealed to Berry on a personal level as well, because she is also of mixed race. When it aired over two nights in February, *The Wedding* received good reviews and drew 24.4 million viewers, more than any other television movie that month.

The Wedding was just the first of many big events for Oprah in 1998. She also received two significant honors: the National Academy of Television Arts and Sciences, which administers the Daytime Emmy Awards, gave Oprah a Lifetime Achievement Award, and *Time* magazine named her one of the 100 Most Influential People of the 20th Century.

On November 14 Oprah made a jubilant return to her hometown in Mississippi in order to open a Habitat for Humanity house that she had funded as part of her Angel Network charity, established the previous year. To help fund the Angel Network, she had asked viewers of her show to save their spare change and send it to the Angel Network so that they could collectively make a difference in the lives of the needy. The resulting donations totaled millions of dollars and were used to fund college scholarships and build homes for low-income families.

Oprah chose to work with Habitat for Humanity, an international organization based in Americus, Georgia, that builds homes for low-income families. The organization also provides interest-free mortgages for those families in exchange for hundreds of hours of "sweat equity"—work they do as a down payment on their new home.

At an informal gathering at the Attala County Coliseum, Oprah announced that she had plans to do even more for the town of Kosciusko, Mississippi. As she handed over the keys of the Habitat for Humanity home to its proud new owners, she told the crowd of about 250 townsfolk, "You have nothing without a home. Everything we are, where we come from, comes from our home. My roots are here. I am who I am because of Kosciusko."

Oprah could afford to be generous. In 1998 *Forbes* magazine rated her as one of the most powerful and wealthy women in the entertainment business, with an estimated income of $125 million a year. She had just renewed her longstanding distribution agreement with King World, which had proven to be a profitable partnership for all parties. Oprah's show accounted for almost 40 percent of King World's annual income. In renewing her contract with the syndication company, the popular television personality agreed to host *The Oprah Winfrey Show* through its 2002 season.

Despite the show's success, when the new television season started in the fall of 1998, Oprah felt she needed to do some fine tuning. "I believe that television can do something it's never done before," she told her viewers. "Do you believe television can change people's lives? Do you believe people really want to change? I'm counting on it. It's not just a new season. I have bigger plans for us."

Those plans included introducing the "Change Your Life TV" format to *The Oprah Winfrey Show*. The new format showcased a panel of experts who would discuss whatever the topic of the day was—usually something that audience members and viewers could use to improve their lives. The last five minutes of each show were dedicated to what Oprah called, "Remembering Your Spirit." The response was mixed. The *Chicago Tribune* lamented the new format, claiming that Oprah was "pushing her agenda like a missionary of personal growth set loose among underimproved natives." The

The Angel Network

Amanda Du... & ...rlotte Church   No. 0023

PAY TO THE ORDER OF The Angel Network $ 100,000.00

One Hundred Thousand Dollars and ——— 00/100 DOLLARS

newspaper labeled her "Deepak Oprah," comparing her to self-help guru Deepak Chopra. Other media experts agreed with the assessment, but Oprah's fans remained unmoved by the critics. They continued to support and watch her show.

The new direction for Oprah's syndicated program was only the first of a series of creative ventures that she initiated that fall. She also announced that Harpo Productions would join the company Oxygen Media in developing a new women-oriented cable network. Oxygen Cable Network was scheduled to launch in February 2000, and would feature Harpo-produced programming. "What I bring to the mix is the absolute connection to the viewer," Oprah said when asked about her role in the project. "I feel it, they feel it, we all know that's what it is. If we can create on this network what we've been able to create on the *Oprah* show, then we'll be highly successful. If we can create

Oprah established the Angel Network, a charity that provides scholarships and low-income housing, by asking viewers of her television program to donate their spare change. Millions of dollars poured in. Here singer Charlotte Church (right) and teen artist Amanda Dunbar (left) surprise the talk-show host with a $100,000 contribution to the charity.

not just credibility but a trust between the audience and ourselves, then we've got it."

Oprah would host two new shows on the network and be involved with its overall programming. Asked whether this new venture would allow her to continue *The Oprah Winfrey Show,* she replied: "I've always made all my decisions based on my gut. My gut told me it was time to leave Baltimore. My gut will tell me whether to continue the show or not. And creating a network that has the best interests of women at heart—well, that's what I try to do every day. It's such a fit."

Starting a cable network is a risky proposition, but Oprah would rather attempt big projects and fail than refuse to do something because it might not work.

At the same time, Oprah finished years of work to bring Toni Morrison's critically acclaimed novel *Beloved* to the big screen. Inspired by the true story of Margaret Garner, a slave who in 1851 tried to kill her children rather than let them be taken back into slavery, *Beloved* tells the fictional story of Sethe, a former slave. She lives with the memories of slavery and of having murdered her daughter, referred to only as "Beloved."

Oprah first read Morrison's book in 1987 and was captivated by the character of Sethe. "I knew Sethe, when I encountered her I felt that she was in some way a part of myself," she explained. On the Saturday that she finished reading the book, Oprah contacted Toni Morrison and asked her for the movie rights. Morrison thought it would be impossible to transfer the story to film, but Oprah convinced her that it could be done and that Oprah Winfrey was the person who could do it.

"My original intention in making *Beloved,*" Oprah later recalled, "was the same as Toni Morrison's intention in writing the book: I wanted people to be able to feel deeply on a very personal level what it meant to be a slave, what slavery did to a people, and also to be liberated by that knowledge." In order to make that vision reality, Oprah collected a highly talented group to work on the

The 1998 movie Beloved *made Oprah especially proud. In this scene, Paul D., played by Danny Glover, embraces Sethe, Oprah's character.*

movie, including renowned director Jonathan Demme and accomplished actor Danny Glover.

Oprah herself played the role of Sethe and took extreme measures to understand the character, including participating in a reenactment in which she portrayed a slave who escaped to freedom. "Slavery was about having no power whatsoever," she wrote the day after the experience. "That's what became so real to me yesterday. . . . I briefly glimpsed the reality of NO choice. It was deadening. It was so painful. I didn't want to feel it. Not even in that controlled, contrived space. So deep. So real. So much pain."

The results of Oprah's preparation were impressive. Demme was initially concerned that people watching the film would see Oprah rather than Sethe on the screen. But those doubts quickly vanished. "While watching the movie," the director commented after the film was completed, "I find myself sometimes literally searching Sethe's face for the Oprah Winfrey we all know so vividly as the *Major Public Figure*, and I can't find her there."

While Oprah herself received critical acclaim for her role as Sethe, the movie did not do well at the box office when it was released in October 1998. Some observers attributed the movie's poor showing to a reluctance on the part of Americans to face the nation's history of racism and slavery. Regardless of whether the movie was successful or not, Oprah has said that she will never love any project the way she did *Beloved*.

Oprah's fans obviously loved her and kept her program at the top of the ratings. By 1999 *The Oprah Winfrey Show* had received a total of 32 Emmy Awards, six of which were individual awards for Oprah as host. The year also marked a change in the syndication of Oprah's program. King World, which had distributed *The Oprah Winfrey Show* since its national debut in 1986, announced that it was being bought by CBS, which was taking over the show's distribution.

Oprah chose this time to withdraw her name from consideration for future Emmy nominations, noting that she had received the lifetime achievement honor the year before. "After you've achieved it for a lifetime," she explained, "what else is there?"

Besides, the energetic woman was busy with other projects. Along with planning her daily television program and developing the Oxygen Cable Network, in 1999 Oprah announced a deal with Hearst Magazines to publish her own lifestyle magazine. Hearst's editor-in-chief Ellen Levine said that the company decided to go ahead with the publication when they saw the impact Oprah had in print. Scheduled to hit the newsstands in March 2000, the magazine would "mirror Oprah's traditional message of self-affirmation for women," said Levine. "If Martha Stewart's magazine is about beautiful exteriors, this is going to be about beautiful interiors."

To further stretch her wings, in the fall of 1999, Oprah had joined fiancé Stedman Graham in teaching a 10-week class at the Northwestern University J. L. Kellogg Graduate School of Management. Called the Dynamics of Leadership, the class was designed to prompt students to "look inside themselves and find those qualities that will make them better leaders in the community." Stedman was in his third year as adjunct professor at the business school, but Oprah had never taught before.

About 110 students took the class, and some of them confessed to having low expectations. "I thought she did a really good job of not making it into a talk show," one student later commented. "I was expecting it to be 'The Oprah Winfrey Show' at Kellogg." But the new teacher made important contributions. Another student described his two teachers this way: "He sticks to the material we're supposed to be learning, and she provides valuable tangents. She brings the material to life."

In November 1999, the National Book Awards celebrated its 50th anniversary, and the National Book Foundation gave Oprah the 50th Anniversary Gold Medal. The foundation director Neil Baldwin said the medal was an "expression of gratitude—not only on the part of our foundation, but also on behalf of the publishing community and the millions of readers whose lives have been enriched by Winfrey's enthusiasm for books."

As she faced a new millennium, Oprah Winfrey epitomized the values of self-knowledge and personal development that her television program, charitable causes, and other activities advocated. Now she was still determined to bring that message to as many people as was humanly possible.

The phenomenal success of The Oprah Winfrey Show, *which regularly draws guests such as popular singer and actress Bette Midler (left), has presented Oprah with opportunities to expand her influence.*

8

NEW WORLDS
TO CONQUER

The year 2000 was full of possibilities for Oprah Winfrey. Although doubters had told her that changing the format of her show would never work, and for a short time viewership was down slightly, *The Oprah Winfrey Show* still remained number one and had never been stronger. The *Los Angeles Times* reported that more than 22 million Americans watched her show every day, and it was viewed in 160 foreign countries. It had become the highest-rated talk show of all time.

Because of Oprah's lucrative syndication agreement, the continuing success of her talk show produced ever-larger financial rewards. Early in 2000, *Forbes* magazine estimated Oprah's personal worth at $670 million. At the end of June, the *Los Angeles Times* had raised that figure to $725 million, and by the end of October, the *Chicago Sun-Times* was reporting her net worth at an even $800 million. Any of those figures would have been unimaginable to the lonely, abused girl growing up on the streets of Milwaukee 35 years earlier.

Everything the woman touched seemed to turn to gold. When the premiere issue of *O* magazine, Oprah's lifestyle magazine, was released that spring, Hearst Magazines was determined to make it a success. The company bought space for the new publication in 50,000 supermarket racks across the nation, resulting in 1.6 million copies sold. Readers sent in more than 500,000 subscription orders. After the first four issues had hit the stands, 75 percent of the copies had sold, an incredibly high figure in a world where the most successful magazines only sell 50 percent of the copies offered on newsstands. The first two issues of *O* eventually sold out.

Why did the magazine enjoy such success? Obviously part of the answer is Oprah herself. "Oprah is a drug for millions of women," said Samir Husni, a professor of media studies at the University of Mississippi. "They need to be reassured, and told that everything is O.K. She does that, and if she does it once a month, she can do it twice a month, and the women will still come running. And Hearst needs to keep praying and lighting candles that the good Lord will add years and years to Oprah's life."

Another part of the magazine's success is its content. Unlike other women's magazines that focus on fashion, home decorating, or simplistic answers to complicated problems, *O* deals with issues familiar to the legions of women who faithfully watch *The Oprah Winfrey Show.* Offering everything from advice on relationships to words of wisdom about becoming a better person, the magazine treats women's issues more seriously than much of its competition.

The magazine also features insights from some of the show's regular guests, such as psychologist Phil McGraw, financial expert Suze Orman, and exercise physiologist Bob Greene. Like most other women's magazines, *O* includes interviews with celebrities, but the people who tell their stories in *O* discuss personal issues more openly. For example, in an article on Oscar-winning actor Sidney Poitier, he discusses the pain he felt in the 1960s when he was ridiculed by some civil rights activists as an Uncle Tom.

Oprah tirelessly promoted the premiere issue of O magazine at events such as this press breakfast in New York City, held two days before the magazine debuted. Her efforts were rewarded when the first issue of the magazine sold out.

While *O* magazine continued to be successful, the Oxygen Cable Network faced a bumpier road. It debuted on February 2, 2000, a date chosen because its numerical representation (02/02) resembles the scientific symbol for an oxygen molecule (O_2). But while *O* magazine appeared to have a clear mission, the goals of Oxygen seemed to be constantly changing. Its initial self-proclaimed vision was to be "a revolution led by women and kids," but the question of where that revolution would lead remained unanswered. From a business stand-point, the fledgling cable network faced a significant problem because it was not readily available in large markets such as Los Angeles and New York City. It also was prohibitively expensive for most smaller cable companies to carry.

The Oxygen Cable Network is a smaller part of Oxygen Media, a company that combines cable television with the Internet. Oxygen's homepage on the Internet includes connections to Oprah's own website and may play a role in increasing subscriber demand for cable companies to carry the network.

It remains to be seen whether Oxygen Cable Network will survive in a highly competitive environment or how much input Oprah will continue to have in this venture. In the meantime, the media executive is busy with another rapidly expanding business. Not only is she involved in determining the content of daily television shows, cable television programs, magazine articles, and Internet websites, but during the summer of 2000 she also began holding seminars called Personal Growth Summits in various U.S. cities. The 5,000 seats available for each of the seminars in Los Angeles, Detroit, and Atlanta sold out within one week of their announcement.

Oprah has agreed to continue producing *The Oprah Winfrey Show* through 2004, but she has reduced the number of new shows to be taped each season, which will give her more time for her other ventures. Through Harpo Productions, she remains involved in producing television movies. In 2000 *Oprah Winfrey Presents: Tuesdays with Morrie,* a film adaptation of the book by the same title, earned an Emmy Award for Outstanding Made-for-Television Movie.

Oprah's foray into teaching was such a success that she agreed to teach another course with Stedman Graham, to whom she remains engaged. The couple keeps tight-lipped about future wedding plans, although rumors of their "impending" marriage circulate regularly.

After decades of struggle, Oprah has reached a level of satisfaction with her life and a true sense of mission.

Oprah remains grateful for what she has accomplished and believes she is an example of what one person can achieve even when confronted by overwhelming odds.

She explained it to one reporter this way: "I was raised with an outhouse, no plumbing. Nobody had any clue that my life could be anything but working in some factory or a cotton field in Mississippi. I feel strongly that my life is to be used as an example to show people what can be done."

In another interview she admitted, "I am finally at a point in my life where I'm doing the kind of shows I've always wanted to do, helping people to see themselves more clearly and to make choices that lead to more fulfilled lives."

The woman who started life facing what appeared to be insurmountable obstacles has accomplished more than most people dream possible. And as Oprah Winfrey looks to the future, rest assured that no one can place limits on what she may yet achieve.

CHRONOLOGY

1954   Born January 29 in Kosciusko, Mississippi; raised by grandparents Hattie Mae and Earless Lee

1960   Moves to Milwaukee, Wisconsin, to live with her mother, Vernita Lee, and half-sister, Patricia; half-brother, Jeffrey, is born

1962   Moves to Nashville, Tennessee, to live with her father, Vernon Winfrey, and her stepmother, Zelma

1963   Moves back to Milwaukee with her mother

1968   Is sent back to Nashville to live with her father

1971   Hired as part-time newscaster at radio station WVOL in Nashville; graduates from East High School; wins Miss Fire Prevention beauty pageant; enters Tennessee State University (TSU)

1972   Wins Miss Black Nashville beauty pageant; wins Miss Black Tennessee beauty pageant; competes in Miss Black America pageant

1973   Accepts job as coanchor of weekend news at CBS affiliate WTVF-TV in Nashville and becomes Nashville's first African American and first woman to anchor television news; continues classes at TSU

1976   Moves to Baltimore, Maryland, to coanchor news at ABC affiliate WJZ-TV

1977   Becomes cohost of WJZ-TV talk show *People Are Talking*

1983   Moves to Chicago and takes job as host of *A.M. Chicago* on WLS-TV

1985   Plays role of Sofia in Steven Spielberg's movie *The Color Purple*; *A.M. Chicago* name changes to *The Oprah Winfrey Show*

1986   Nominated for Academy Award as Best Supporting Actress for her role in *The Color Purple*; *The Oprah Winfrey Show* premiers as a nationally syndicated program; begins dating Stedman Graham; forms Harpo Productions to produce and develop television and movie projects

1987   Completes requirements for and receives degree from TSU; endows 10 scholarships in her father's name at the school

1989   Produces television movie *The Women of Brewster Place*, the first movie by Harpo Productions; half-brother, Jeffrey Lee, dies from AIDS

1991   Testifies before the Senate Judiciary Committee and tries unsuccessfully to get the National Child Protection Act passed into law

1992   Hosts "Scared Silent," a television documentary about child abuse; announces engagement to Stedman Graham; interviews Michael Jackson for primetime special

CHRONOLOGY

1993   National Child Protection Act passes both houses of Congress

1994   Enters and completes the Marine Corps Marathon in Washington, D.C.; staff problems plague *The Oprah Winfrey Show*; Oprah decides to change program's direction

1995   During taping of *The Oprah Winfrey Show*, acknowledges previous drug use; *Runner's World* magazine puts Oprah on the cover

1996   Forms Oprah's Book Club; releases book *Make the Connection: Ten Steps to a Better Body and a Better Life*, cowritten with trainer Bob Greene

1997   Lawsuit filed against Oprah by Texas ranchers; Oprah founds the charity Angel Network

1998   Wins cattlemen lawsuit; coproduces and stars in movie *Beloved*; Harpo Productions joins with Oxygen Media to create a cable network channel, Oxygen

1999   Works with Hearst Magazines to develop *O* magazine; teaches 10-week graduate class in management at Northwestern University with fiancé Stedman Graham

2000   Launches Oxygen Cable Network and *O* magazine; continues teaching at Northwestern University; extends contract for *The Oprah Winfrey Show* through 2004

AWARDS

1986   Emmy Award for Outstanding Talk/Service Show Host

1987   Broadcaster of the Year Award from the International Radio and Television Society

1990   Emmy Award for Outstanding Talk/Service Show Host

1991   Emmy Award for Outstanding Talk/Service Show Host

Humanitarian Award from the Jesse Owens Foundation

1992   Emmy Award for Outstanding Talk/Service Show Host

1993   Emmy Award for Outstanding Talk Show Host

Horatio Alger Award

1994   Emmy Award for Outstanding Talk Show Host

Inducted into National Academy of Television Arts and Sciences Hall of Fame

Best Foreign Television Program for *The Oprah Winfrey Show* from the British Academy of Film and Television Arts

1996   George Foster Peabody Individual Achievement Award

1998   Lifetime Achievement Award from the National Academy of Television Arts and Sciences

Time magazine 100 Most Influential People of the 20th Century

1999   50th Anniversary Gold Medal from National Book Foundation

2000   Emmy Award for Outstanding Made-for-Television Movie for *Oprah Winfrey Presents: Tuesdays with Morrie*

Avins, Mimi. "Flocking to the Church of Oprah." *Los Angeles Times*,
   25 June 2000.

"Backing off from the Book." *People*, 5 July 1993.

Bark, Ed. "Making Time for the Prime: Peabody Awards Honor the Best of
   Television." *Dallas Morning News*, 7 May 1996.

Calkins, Laurel Brubaker. "Oprah 1, Beef 0: A Texas Jury Steers Winfrey to
   Victory in a Meaty Libel Case." *People*, 16 March 1998.

Clemetson, Lynette. "The Birth of a Network." *Newsweek*,
   15 November 1999.

Cohen, Adam. "Trial of the Savory." *Time*, 2 February 1998.

Cohen, David. "Oprah Returns to College: This Time as Subject for a
   Course." *Chicago Sun-Times*, 7 May 2000.

Cotton, C. Richard. "Oprah Amazes Hometown with Largess: Looks Like More
   to Come." *Memphis (Tenn.) Commercial Appeal*, 15 November 1998.

Donovan, Lisa, and Tom Ragan. "'Professor' Winfrey Steps up to the Head
   of Grad Class at NU." *Chicago Tribune*, 29 September 1999.

D'Orio, Wayne. "Creating Oprah: The Magazine." *Folio*, 1 September 1999.

Due, Tananarive. "Oprah Shares Her Struggle to Lose Weight in New
   Video." *Knight-Ridder/Tribune News Service*, 2 October 1997.

Edwards, Ellen. "Oprah Winfrey Admits Drug Use During Taping: TV Host
   Confesses She Smoked Cocaine." *Washington Post*, 13 January 1995.

"Emmy Awards." *Chicago Sun-Times*, 11 November 2000.

Farrell, Mary H. J., Katy Kelly, and Barbara Kleban Mills. "Oprah's Crusade."
   People, 2 December 1991.

Fitch, Jessica Madore. "Oprah Winfrey, 46." *Chicago Sun-Times*,
   29 October 2000.

Greene, Bob, and Oprah Winfrey. *Make the Connection: Ten Steps to a Better
   Body and a Better Life*. New York: Hyperion, 1996.

Hodges, Ann. "Oprah Winfrey's Wedding Invitation." *Houston (Tex.)
   Chronicle*, 20 February 1998.

Hofmeister, Sallie. "CBS to Acquire 'Oprah' Syndicator King World."
   Los Angeles Times, 2 April 1999.

Jarvis, Jeff. "Top 10 Oprahs." *People Weekly*, 5 September 1988.

BIBLIOGRAPHY

Johnson, Marilyn, and Dana Fineman. "Oprah Winfrey: A Life in Books." *Life*, September 1997.

Johnson, Steve. "Oh, No Oprah! Enough!" *Chicago Tribune*, 23 November 1998.

King, Norman. *Everybody Loves Oprah! Her Remarkable Life Story.* New York: William Morrow, 1987.

Kuczynski, Alex. "Oprah, Coast to Coast; A Phenomenon Struts Her Stuff on the Newsstand." *New York Times*, 2 October 2000.

Littlefield, Kinney. "Oprah Opens Up." *Santa Ana (Calif.) Orange County Register*, 14 May 1997.

Lowe, Janet. *Oprah Winfrey Speaks: Insight from the World's Most Influential Voice.* New York: John Wiley, 1998.

Mair, George. *Oprah Winfrey: The Real Story.* New York: Birch Lane Press, 1994.

Max, D. T. "No Wonder Everyone Loves Oprah Winfrey's Book Club." *London Guardian*, 4 January 2000.

Mitchell, Peter. "Texas Beef Farmers Lose Food-Libel Battle with Oprah." *Lancet*, 14 March 1998.

"NBA to Mark 50th Year: Will Award Medal to Oprah." *Publishers Weekly*, 7 June 1999.

Nicholson, Lois P. *Oprah Winfrey*. Philadelphia: Chelsea House Publishers, 1994.

Noden, Merrell. *People Profiles: Oprah Winfrey.* New York: Time Inc., 1999.

O'Brien, Maureen. "Oprah Winfrey Shock: The Big Fall Book That Vanished." *Publishers Weekly*, 21 June 1993.

"Old Power." *Economist*, 5 February 2000.

"Oprah Gives $1 Million to Spelman College's Science Fund." *Jet*, 27 November 1995.

"Oprah to Make Fewer New Shows." *Chicago Sun-Times*, 11 November 2000.

"Oprah Winfrey Responds to Allegations that Her Father Harassed College Student." *Jet*, 20 February 1995.

"Oprah Winfrey to Receive the Horatio Alger Award." *Jet*, 1 February 1993.

"Oprah Withdraws as Nominee in Daytime Emmys' Best Talk Show Host

Category." *Jet*, 22 March 1999.

"Oprah's Going Glossy." *Newsweek*, 19 July 1999.

Pitts, Leonard Jr. "The Queen of Gab Leads a Campaign Against Sleaze TV." *Knight-Ridder/Tribune News Service*, 20 July 1995.

Rampton, Sheldon and John Stauber. "Shut Up and Eat: The Lessons of the Oprah Trial." *Nation*, 16 February 1998.

Richman, Alan. "Oprah: TV's Queen of Talk Has a Hit Show, a New Man and a Peeve: 'I Hate Being Called Fat.'" *People*, 12 January 1987.

Reynolds, Gretchen. "The Oprah Winfrey Plan." *Runner's World*, March 1995.

Rickey, Carrie. "Oprah Winfrey Gets to Say in 'Beloved' What She's Tried to Say on TV for Years." *Philadelphia Inquirer*, 9 October 1998.

Rowe, Patricia. "Child Abuse Telecast Floods National Hotline." *Children Today*, March–April 1992.

"TV News & Notes: Oprah Signs New Contract Through 2003–2004 Season." *Atlanta Journal and Constitution*, 3 November 2000.

Waldron, Robert. *Oprah!* New York: St. Martin's, 1987.

Walsh, Sharon. "Oxygen Loses Some of Its Air." *Industry Standard*, 21 August 2000.

Whitaker, Charles. "TV's New Daytime Darling." *Saturday Evening Post*, July–August 1987.

Winfrey, Oprah. *Journey to Beloved*. New York: Hyperion, 1998.

WEB SITES

Online with Oprah
www.oprah.com

Child Abuse Prevention Network
www.child-abuse.com

National Association of Broadcasters
www.nab.org

Literacy Volunteers of America
www.literacyvolunteers.org

INDEX

ABC network
  and Harpo Productions,
    67-68
  and *The Wedding*, 87-89
Abrams, Gene, 23
Academy Award nominations,
  for *The Color Purple*, 15
Affirmative action, 36
All My Children (TV soap
  opera), 47, 49
A.M. Chicago (TV talk show),
  13, 49-51, 53-56
  *See also Oprah Winfrey
  Show, The*
Angel Network charity, 89
Angelou, Maya, 25
Athletes Against Drugs, 57

Baker, Bill, 46, 47
Baldwin, Neil, 95
Baltimore, Maryland, 42-49
B&C Associates, 57
Beloved (film), 92-94
Berry, Halle, 87, 89
Better Chance, A (ABC),
  82-83
Biden, Joseph, 72
Brewster Place (TV series),
  67-68
Brown, Gordon, 34
Bumpas, Gayle King,
  45, 48
Burch, Janet, 35, 36
Burfoot, Amby, 78

Cannon, Reuben, 13, 14
Chapman, Harry, 41-42
Chicago, Illinois, 49-51
Clark, Chris, 39, 40-41,
  42
Clinton, Bill, 75
Cole, Johnnetta, 81
Color Purple, The (film),
  13-15, 56, 67
Cosby, Bill, 73
Cox, William, 33, 41

Demme, Jonathan, 93

DiMaio, Debra, 45-46, 49,
  59, 80
Donahue, Phil, and *Donahue*
  (TV talk show), 46, 50,
  53-54, 55, 56, 59-61

East High School (Nashville),
  27-32
Engler, Paul, 84
Esters, Katherine Carr
  (cousin), 19

False Disparagement of
  Perishable Food Products
  Act, 84
Families for a Better Life,
  75-76
Federal Communications
  Commission (FCC), 36
Fishburne, Laurence, 14

Garner, Margaret, 92
Geraldo (TV talk show), 80
Glover, Danny, 14, 93
Goldberg, Whoopie, 14
Graham, Stedman (boyfriend)
  as college teacher, 95
  and engagement to
    Oprah, 74
  and first meeting with
    Oprah, 57-58
  and "impending" marriage
    to Oprah, 100
Grauman's Chinese Theatre,
  Walk of Stars of, 28
Greene, Bob, 74, 77, 78, 82
Group W Production, 48

Habitat for Humanity, 89-90
Harpo Productions, 57, 65
  and ABC, 67-68
  and *Brewster Place*, 67-68
  building purchased for, 65
  formation of, 57
  and Oxygen Cable Network,
    91-92, 94, 99-100
  and *The Women of Brewster
    Place* (TV film), 67

See also Oprah Winfrey
  Presents
Hearst Magazines, and *O*
  magazine, 94, 97-99
Heidelberg, John, 29-30,
  31
Holt, Gary, 27, 28
Honors and awards
  Academy of Television
    Arts and Sciences Hall
    of Fame, 78
  beauty pageant titles,
    31-32, 33-36
  Best Foreign Television
    Program from British
    Academy of Film and
    Television Arts, 78
  Broadcaster of the Year
    Award from Interna-
    tional Radio and
    Television Society, 61
  Daytime Emmy Awards
    hostess, 61
  Emmy Awards for
    Outstanding Talk/
    Service Show Host,
    61, 74, 94
  50th Anniversary Gold
    Medal from National
    Book Foundation, 95
  George Foster Peabody
    Individual Achievement
    Award, 82
  Horatio Alger Award
    from Horatio Alger
    Association of Distin-
    guished Americans, 76
  Humanitarian Award
    from Jesse Owens
    Foundation, 73
  Lifetime Achievement
    Award from National
    Academy of Television
    Arts and Sciences, 89
  Most Popular Girl in high
    school class, 31
  Outstanding Teenager of
    America, 28

Time magazine 100 Most Influential People of the 20th Century, 89
White House Conference on Youth, 28
Humane Society of the United States, 84
Husni, Samir, 98

Jackson, Michael, 73-74
Jacobs, Jeffrey, 57
Jarvis, Jeff, 62
Johnson, Suzanne, 57
Jones, Quincy, 13

Kennedy, Pamela, 81-82
Kern, Art, 47-48
Kilcrese, Clarence, 30-31
King World Productions, 56-57, 58-59, 90, 94
Kosciusko, Mississippi
    Oprah's childhood in, 17, 18, 24
    and Oprah's donation to Habitat for Humanity, 89-90
Kościusko, Tadeusz Andrzei Bonawentura, 17
Kupcinet, Irv, 73

Lee, Earless (grandfather), 18, 20, 24
Lee, Hattie Mae (grandmother), 18-19, 20, 24
Lee, Jeffrey (half-brother), 20, 65, 67
Lee, Patricia (half-sister), 20, 25, 67
Lee, Vernita (mother), 17-18, 19, 20-23, 24, 65, 67
Levine, Ellen, 94
Lincoln Middle School (Milwaukee), 23
Lyman, Howard, 84

Make the Connection: Ten Steps to a Better Body and a Better Life (book), 82-83

March of Dimes walkathon, 29-30
Marine Corps Marathon, 78
Maurice, Dick, 47
McGraw, Phil, 98
Mena, Angelica, 71-73
Milwaukee, Wisconsin, 20-24
Miss Black America beauty pageant, 35-36
Miss Black Nashville beauty pageant, 33-34
Miss Black Tennessee beauty pageant, 34-35
Miss Fire Prevention beauty pageant, 31-32
Morehouse College, Oprah's gift to, 73
Morrison, Toni, 92

Nashville, Tennessee, 21, 24-25, 27-32, 44
National Child Protection Act, 72-73, 75
Nicolet High School (Milwaukee), 23-24, 27
Nixon, Richard, 28
Northwestern University, 95

O magazine, 94, 97-99
Oprah's Book Club, 82-83
Oprah Winfrey Presents
    and *Tuesdays with Morrie*, 100
    and *The Wedding*, 87-89
Oprah Winfrey Show, The, 56-57, 59-62, 67, 74, 82-85
    from Amarillo, Texas, 85
    changes in programming of, 80-81
    "Change Your Life TV" format for, 90-91
    critics of, 62, 67, 90-91
    Donahue versus, 50, 53-54, 56, 59-61

Emmy Awards received by, 61, 94
from Forsyth County, Georgia, 60-61
and lawsuit by Texas ranchers, 83-85
and Oprah's Book Club, 82-83
and "sleaze TV," 80-81, 85
staff problems at, 79-80
success of, 59-61, 94, 97
syndication of, 56-57, 58-59, 90, 94, 97
Orman, Suze, 98
Otey, Anthony, 31
Oxygen Cable Network, 91-92, 94, 99-100

Palley, Stephen W., 59
Payne, Les, 59
People Are Talking (TV talk show), 46-48
Personal Growth Summits (seminars), 100
Poitier, Sidney, 98

Raleigh, Colleen, 79-80
Ricki Lake (TV talk show), 80
Rivers, Joan, 14, 55-56
Runner's World (magazine), 78

"Scared Silent: Exposing Child Abuse" (TV documentary), 74-75
Selleck, Tom, 53
Senate Judiciary Committee, 72
Sexual abuse, 23, 24-25, 69, 71-73, 74-75
Shapiro, Arnold, 75
Sher, Richard, 47
Spelman College, 81
Spielberg, Steven, 14, 56
Swanson, Dennis, 50, 53

INDEX

Tennessee State University
(TSU)
  Oprah as student at,
    32-33, 36, 41, 42
  Oprah's endowment to,
    62, 81-82
Texas ranchers, and lawsuit
  against Oprah, 83-85
There Are No Children Here
  (TV film), 75-76
Thomas, Marlo, 55
Thompson, James, 72
*Tonight Show with Johnny
  Carson, The* (TV appear-
  ance), 14, 55-56
Tuesdays with Morrie
  (TV film), 100
Turner, Jerry, 43, 44

Upward Bound, 23

Waldron, Robert, 36
Walker, Alice, 13, 14
Wallace, Mike, 44
Walters, Barbara, 39, 42
Wedding, The (TV miniseries),
  87-89
West, Dorothy, 87
Williams, Hosea, 60
Winfrey, Oprah
  as actress, 15, 33, 49, 67,
    75-76, 92-94
  and autobiography, 76-77
  in Baltimore, 42-49
  and beauty pageants,
    31-32, 33-36
  birth of, 17
  and cattlemen lawsuit,
    83-85
  and charities, 62, 73, 75-
    76, 81, 82-83, 89-90
  in Chicago, 49-51
  Chicago home of, 57
  childhood of, 15, 17-23
  and church, 19, 20, 21,
    25, 28, 33

as college teacher, 95, 100
and drug use, 81
education of, 19-20, 21,
  23-24, 25, 27-32, 33,
  41, 42, 62
family of, 17-19, 20-23,
  24-25, 44, 65, 67
friendships of, 45-46, 48,
  49, 57, 59, 80
in Kosciusko, 17, 18, 24
lifestyle of, 57, 62-64
and magazine, 95, 97-99
in Milwaukee, 20-24
in Nashville, 21, 24-25,
  27-32, 44
as news coanchor, 36-37,
  39-44
outlook of, 15, 100-101
as part-time newscaster,
  29-31, 33
pregnancy of, 25
and prime-time interview
  with Michael Jackson,
  73-74
and racism, 17, 27, 28,
  32-33, 36-37, 41,
  60-61
relationships of, 31,
  48-49. *See also* Graham,
  Stedman
seminars of, 100
and sexual abuse, 23,
  24-25, 69, 71-73,
  74-75
and single mothers, 75-76
in soap opera, 49
as spot reporter, 44-46
and suicide, 48
and talent, 19, 20, 21, 23,
  28-31, 32, 33-36
as talk-show cohost,
  46-48
as talk-show host,
  13, 49-51, 53-56.
  *See also Oprah Winfrey
  Show, The*

teenage years of, 23-25,
  27-32
and TV movies. *See*
  Harpo Productions;
  Oprah Winfrey Presents
wealth of, 57, 90, 97
and weight problem,
  14, 48, 49, 54-56, 57,
  65, 68-69, 74, 76-78,
  82-83
Winfrey, Vernon (father)
  and *The Color Purple*, 15
  and lawsuit over sexual
    advances, 15, 81-82
  and Oprah as part-time
    newscaster, 31
  and Oprah's birth, 17-18
  and Oprah's childhood,
    21-22, 24-25, 32
  and Oprah's education,
    25, 31, 32, 62
  and Oprah's talent, 28
  and scholarships to
    Tennessee State
    University, 62, 81-82
Winfrey, Zelma
  (stepmother), 21, 24,
  25, 32
WJZ-TV and Oprah
  as coanchor, 42-44
  as cohost of *People are
    Talking*, 46-48
  as spot reporter, 44-46
WLS-TV and Oprah
  as host of *A.M. Chicago*,
    49-51, 53-56. *See also
    Oprah Winfrey Show, The*
*Women of Brewster Place,
  The* (TV film), 67
WTVF-TV and Oprah
  as coanchor, 36-37,
    39-42
WVOL and Oprah
  as part-time newscaster,
    29-31, 33

PICTURE CREDITS

Belinda Friedrich is the author of *The Simple Guide to St. Maarten/ St. Martin*. She is studying for a master's degree in counseling from Webster University and lives with her husband, Karl, in Pawleys Island, S.C. She has two sons.

Matina S. Horner was president of Radcliffe College and associate professor of psychology and social relations at Harvard University. She is best known for her studies of women's motivation, achievement, and personality development. Dr. Horner has served on several national boards and advisory councils, including those of the National Science Foundation, Time Inc., and the Women's Research and Education Institute. She earned her B.A. from Bryn Mawr College and her Ph.D. from the University of Michigan, and holds honorary degrees from many colleges and universities, including Mount Holyoke, Smith, Tufts, and the University of Pennsylvania.